The Teachers Speak
Celestial lessons by the Teachers of Peace

Roberta A. Yackel

The Teachers Speak

About the *Teachers of Peace*

*"Home, there are many of us,
where there is perfect Oneness, Home."*

These are the first words spoken by the *Teachers of Peace*. This occurred in 1991 while I was serving as minister of Unity Church in Albany, New York. I did not consciously seek out this celestial contact, however, looking back at my childhood, it is clear to me now that I had been preparing for such an experience from a young age. As a child I didn't feel totally attached to my body until contact with the solidity of the earth intruded upon my world. I remember joyously running and skipping along a country road until I took a hard fall onto gravel. I decided then that I was not going to run anymore because the earth is just too hard!

My spiritual explorations began early as well. When I was seven years old, I spent the whole day asking myself the question, "If Jesus comes for me tonight, will I go with him?" By bedtime I had come to the conclusion that, even though I would miss my parents and siblings, if Jesus came for me I really ought to go with him. Just before falling asleep, I asked my little sister the same question. Years later she told me she spent that night wide awake, terrified that Jesus would come and take her away!

Through my teens I continued to ask questions about life and death. I even gave up chocolate for a whole year! This in an attempt to heal a family friend who had been paralyzed from the neck down. My prayers weren't working so I thought that giving up something I loved might heal him. Sadly, it did not. In my later teens, when holding an object or doing an activity, I would often ask myself "What difference will this make when I'm dead?" I wasn't depressed, I was attempting to determine what is truly important in life. Religion, as I understood spirituality to be at the time, turned out to be the winner. This led me to explore many religious traditions and practices, both Eastern and Western. I eventually settled on Religious Science, a New

Thought Christian denomination that blended the teachings and philosophies of both. When I decided to pursue a career in the ministry, I attended the Unity School of Christianity Ministerial Program at Unity Village near Kansas City Missouri. I graduated and was ordained a Unity Minister in 1987.

While serving in my first ministry, I started to pray the *Prayer of St. Francis*, often called the "Peace Prayer." It begins, "Lord, make me an instrument of your Peace." After some time, I began to feel that a presence was seeking to move through me. After considerable resistance, I surrendered and the *Teachers of Peace* began to speak. We spoke privately at first. As my confidence in them grew, I left my ministerial position and began to share their lessons in a variety of public settings.

I am aware of what I am saying as I channel. I experience my personal, ego self moving over to the right side of my consciousness as the transmission of the *Teachers'* energy and words come through the left side of my consciousness. Sometimes, as evidenced by the recordings of public channelings, the *Teachers* would say, "Give us a moment, Roberta must remove herself." This was a reminder to move my personal self back to the right side of my consciousness and allow the *Teachers* to speak. The presence of the *Teachers of Peace* has not shielded me from the life lessons that are mine to learn, nor do I claim that they contain all truth. Each person must determine their value for themselves. These lessons are offered with love and a sincere desire that they may assist you to experience the Peace of God, a peace that passes all intellectual understanding.

Reverend Roberta Yackel

*This book is dedicated to my sister Christine,
a dear friend in this life and in life after life.*

The Teachers Speak

Celestial lessons by the Teachers of Peace

Lesson 1	Covenant of Peace	7
Lesson 2	Celestial System	15
Lesson 3	Life as a School	23
Lesson 4	The Earth	31
Lesson 5	The Body Vehicle	39
Lesson 6	Relationships	47
Lesson 7	Acceptance	55
Lesson 8	Overcoming Fear	61
Lesson 9	Forgiveness	67
Lesson 10	Good and Evil	75
Lesson 11	Spiritual Teachers	83
Lesson 12	The Spiritual Journey	91
Lesson 13	Questions & Answers	103
Lesson 14	In the Light	119

Copyright 2022 All Rights Reserved
ISBN: 979-8-9867590-0-5

The Teachers Speak

The Peace of God

is all I seek, all

I experience,

all I express.

Lesson 1 - Covenant of Peace

The Teachers Speak

Lesson 1

Covenant of Peace

We wait for the call and when called we are pleased to make ourselves known. We are the teaching group of which Roberta is a part. We are a large collection of souls that have evolved to a particular level of consciousness and our assignment is to teach in the various evolving spheres. You may picture us as a large light. As our speakers in various realms open to our presence, an aspect of us steps forward to try to communicate. We are the main speaker for Roberta; however, she has sometimes experienced slightly different energies.

Our purpose in communicating through a speaker is to bring to your awareness the existence of realms that are greater than your normal waking consciousness. In your world, there is belief in other realms such as heaven, however, there is little evidence coming forth to support this belief. It is important that the evidence be felt and known because only believing is no longer adequate in terms of your understanding. When you have the perspective that there are many, many levels of consciousness, your life on the earth will take on a new meaning.

Each one of you is a member of a Spiritual Family. You understand these many levels of consciousness in a linear fashion. In other words, as some Spiritual Families being more evolved than others. However, this is not how it is from our perspective. Spiritual Families are simply a matter of different aspects, different ways of reaching the same goal, which is complete union with the Creator. As part of her Spiritual Family, Roberta's assignment is to be a bridge to a greater reality by giving evidence of the existence of that higher reality.

You are here and you are there simultaneously. You are focused in this physical reality and at the same time your Essence is connected to the Spiritual Family through which you evolve. You each have a particular quality through which your evolution is best expressed. For example, Roberta's quality is peace and our focus with her is the Peace of God. For others, the focus may be on love and forgiveness as in the Jesus Christ Spiritual Family or, it may be through another aspect such as joy or strength. Not all of the aspects are what you would call positive from an earthly point of view. For example, there are groups that evolve through struggle and others that evolve through conflict. All of these aspects exist without judgment in the universal context. They are simply tools through which the soul's evolution is assured.

We will speak to you this day about the Peace of God. The world cries for peace, yet it denies itself the peace it seeks. The world seeks peace where it cannot be found. The people of the world desire peace, however, they will not relinquish their armor nor cast aside their appliances of warfare. Peace cannot be found within the longings of the human race. Peace is found within the total acceptance of God. How many individuals accept the Creator totally and unconditionally? There are so few. There are perhaps twenty individuals on your planet at the present time who know the peace the world is seeking. They assist those who are ready to join them to experience the bliss of true peace. How can the world be peaceful when so few are in possession of the Peace of God? This is why peace on earth cannot yet occur. Celestial beings cannot make you experience such bliss, this wondrous gift of the Creator. We can, however, show you that it exists.

To attain the Peace of God you must seek and
desire it beyond all other things.

This we do not say lightly. The majority of individuals in your world have not been sufficiently convinced that the things of the world are powerless to bring them the happiness and peace they innately desire. Therefore, practicing true peace is left up to the few individuals who fully understand that the promises of the world are false promises and the glitter of the world is temporary and deceiving. If you have begun to understand these things, you are a candidate to experience what we call the Peace of God.

You will be required to release many things. You will be required to sacrifice many ideas. You will be required to seek the Peace of God above all else. You will be required to surrender yourself to the Creator entirely. These are the determining factors. You will find, as the journey unfolds, many individuals who began the journey with you will stop due to their fear, doubt and personal preferences. You will have to lovingly release them.

Consider your commitment to this path of peace carefully. It is not a path of pleasure; it is not a path of convenience; it is not a path of security; it is not a path of contentment. It is a path that requires all you have. It is a path that requires more than you are aware that you have. Be mindful that to seek the Peace of God is a serious pursuit. Be mindful that to attain such bliss is the greatest achievement, the greatest gift, the greatest experience you can know within your present context. Be advised that as a person of peace, much will be asked of you and much will be given forth from you. However, all will be given to you and thus, there will be no end to your ability to give.

Peace is not the absence of war, peace is the acceptance of God.
Peace comes like a thief in the night. It steals your dilemma and
diminishes your darkness. Seek peace and allow it
to destroy your defenses against God.

Covenant of Peace

The Covenant of Peace is given to every soul created by the Creator. The Covenant of Peace is a promise. This promise is unbreakable and intrinsic in nature. It is a bond of love greater than the bond between a parent and child. It is a bond of parent and child in the highest sense. Your Creator loves you, its creation, with a love unknown on earth. The Creator's love is like a vast ocean in which you are set free to grow and evolve, while always suspended within the embrace of this ocean of love. The Covenant of Peace is a promise of enduring presence as you take the journey from unconsciousness to consciousness, from infancy to adulthood, from ignorance to bliss.

You spend many lifetimes in ignorance yet, even as you do, the promise of the Creator's peace and love is evident. Many of your experiences within such lifetimes are misunderstood and even blamed on the Creator and yet, the abiding love of the Covenant of Peace remains. Many lives are lived in want, fear and despair and yet, the Covenant of Peace remains. Many acts of brutality and hatred are performed by the children of the Creator and yet, the Covenant of Peace remains. No act, no matter how despicable, can break this promise of love and peace between the Creator and its offspring. The darkness mankind weaves throughout his history separates them from the awareness of the Covenant of Peace and yet, it cannot erase this bond of love nor its purpose.

The Covenant of Peace is indestructible.

Eventually, through much trial and error, each soul begins to glimpse the truth of this promise. The soul then begins to see a flicker of light on the far horizon and the journey toward conscious union with the Creator begins in earnest. This is the beginning of the spiritual journey. This journey could not exist without the bond between the Creator and its offspring. The light once seen, if only for an instant, can never be diminished or ignored. The light once seen becomes a magnet, a most positive obsession, a point of reference in an otherwise desperate existence. The light once seen is an event that is celebrated by all of the messengers of the Creator. The light once seen is the first recognition of the Covenant of Peace that has existed between the Creator and its creations from the beginning of time.

The journey takes place over millions of years and yet, it is complete in an instant. The reunion of Creator and offspring is never fully accomplished and yet, it always exists. The spiritual journey must be taken and yet, where it leads is truly a mystery. If you have seen the light of the Covenant of Peace you will eventually know all things, experience all things, and be all things. To take this journey you must keep your eye focused on the light, no matter how dim it may seem.

The Covenant of Peace will lead you home to the love, light and peace of your Creator. Stay focused on the spiritual journey, take one step at a time and remember that life is experienced for one purpose and that purpose is to assist you on this journey. The spiritual journey is the only true aspect of your life. Do not forsake it for lesser things that have no substance or real existence. Take the bond of the Covenant, the promise of true peace, into every aspect of your life. Use your life for its intended purpose. Do not waste it gathering objects that have no value beyond the enhancement of your temporary physical existence. If you are reading these words, you have glimpsed greater light and are ready to proceed. Always remember that the promise of the Creator is steadfast. It says, "You cannot be outside of my ocean of love and peace. Therefore, allow me to assist you as you explore, discover and uncover the truth of your being." We are messengers to guide your journey. In the following pages we will speak to you on many subjects. However, remember that all you need to do is seek the experience of the Peace of God.

"Peace, I leave with you, my peace I give to you; not as the world gives do I give to you." (John 14:27)

The Teachers Speak

The messengers

of God are

with you.

Lesson 2 - Celestial System

The Teachers Speak

Lesson 2

The Celestial System

We will speak to you this day about the Celestial System and Spiritual Families. The Celestial System is the Creator's method for the evolution of its creations. In that it has been conceived and brought forth by the Creator, it is perfect in every detail. This perfection can only be understood from a universal perspective. The system consists of many levels of evolutionary beings. These beings have evolved in various worlds, some like your own and many that are very different from your world. As each individual emerges into conscious spiritual evolution, they become aware of the Celestial System. Conscious joining is required to progress. Those of greater spiritual evolution join in vibratory groups. These groups are formed naturally by the process of spiritual growth itself. Each Spiritual Family is a unique vibratory aspect of the Creator. For example, there is a vibratory group known as the Peace of God. We are a part of this group and speak to you from this vibration. There are many other vibratory groups, each one expressing a particular aspect of the Creator. As you evolve in a context such as the earth, you will become more and more aware of the theme of your Spiritual Family. You may be of the vibration of love, the vibration of knowledge, the vibration of selfless service, the vibration of death and rebirth, the vibration of technology and so on. Once an individual evolves through their many incarnations on the earth, they reach a point in their evolution when it is no longer necessary to learn in such a high contrast environment. At this point, the individual continues to learn and grow on other planes, with more subtle vibrations. These vibratory planes cannot be witnessed with physical eyes.

As higher vibratory groups evolve, they also teach.

The theme of learning and teaching continues throughout all vibratory groups and levels. We learn from a vibratory level that is greater in spiritual understanding than we are. We are beyond you in spiritual understanding and therefore our teaching assignment is to assist you. There are many Spiritual Families and thus, there is much assistance available to those of you who are learning and teaching in the dense context of the planet earth. Our role is to assist you. It is not, however, to rescue you or protect you from experiences that bring you greater spiritual evolution. If we were to intervene to protect you from experiences that may be difficult and painful, we would impede your progress. Such intervention would be to your detriment. Thus, evolved beings guide you in a way that ultimately assists you, rather than in a manner that may block your spiritual growth.

Some call unseen spiritual teachers, such as ourselves, angels.

Angels have been witnessed in your context in many different ways, most dramatically when direct intervention takes place. Direct intervention by the angels of God may occur in situations in which the consequences of an experience seriously threaten an individual's ability to remain in the body vehicle. For the most part, however, angels work as messengers in an attempt to bring you higher insight and guidance.

Until an individual is consciously on the spiritual journey, they will have no awareness of the higher assistance available to them. Once an individual sees a glimpse of greater light and begins the conscious spiritual journey, the assistance of the messengers of God becomes more real to them. Sometimes this awareness can cause confusion and an individual may try to relinquish their responsibility for their own life choices. If one does so, difficulties will arise and lessons will be learned. No other being, no matter how highly evolved, can do the work of spiritual evolution for you. However, they can assist you by drawing you up to a more enlightened vibratory level. This is accomplished by simply being present with you and by focusing their attention on you. Your path of spiritual evolution is unique; the lessons you must learn are unique; the lessons you will teach are unique.

Do not seek direct intervention by the Angels of God.

Direct interventions occur only in certain situations and only when absolutely necessary. You must focus on the love of the Creator and on the next step in your spiritual journey. The next step will always be right in front of you, clearly placed in your path. The Messengers of God are with you as you are a part of their vibratory group, your Spiritual Family. You will be best assisted by those of your own vibration.

There are no high or low, good or bad Spiritual Family vibrations; they are different aspects and resonances of the Creator. The Creator is like the sun. It gives off light in every direction. No vibratory group is loved more or less than any other. It is a perfect system for drawing each individual Essence home to the bosom of the Creator. It is a very complex system, one that cannot be fully comprehended by the human mind. You do not need to understand it intellectually, however, you do need to embrace it and consciously seek to enter into it.

You cannot be outside of the Celestial System.

You cannot be outside of the love of the Creator. However, you can be in a state of ignorance and darkness that feels like being outside of the love and light of the Creator. Once you place yourself firmly on the spiritual path, you will begin to see how the system works and you will become a conscious participant in the Creator's plan of redemption. You are not alone in the world; you are not alone in the universe; you are not alone in creation. Those who have gone before you are available to assist you, just as you must be available to assist others.

Do not judge the spiritual evolution of yourself or others. Such judgments have no meaning or purpose. Comparisons do not move you forward but they can temporarily halt your progress. Within the Celestial System there is no good or bad, there is only movement toward the light or resistance to the light. If you wish to aide in your own evolution, release judgments and comparisons as they only serve to create resistance to moving forward. You must accept your current level of spiritual awareness in order to take the next step in the Creator's plan for you. Do not become overwhelmed by the thought of the Celestial System. It is in place and you do not need to do anything except become a willing participant in it. Do not resist the purpose of your existence but cooperate fully with it and allow it to draw you, teach you, assist you and love you.

Many individuals who have begun to understand the availability of Celestial assistance desire a more concrete communication with it. Each one of you has a higher communication faculty that is natural to you. Your faculty may be the ability to hear inner messages, you may be able to receive images in your mind's eye or have a strong sensing ability. Do not, however, seek to cultivate these faculties before you are fully dedicated in service and love to the Creator. If you use psychic techniques to develop inner listening, inner sight or inner knowing before you are fully established in the vibration of the Creator's grace, you may open yourself up to lesser vibratory influences. When lesser influences are drawn to you, you may misinterpret what you receive. You may believe you are receiving assistance from your Spiritual Family, however, you may be receiving confusing and hazardous messages from the astral plane.

The astral plane is a non-physical mirror of the physical universe.

When something manifests in your world, it must move through the astral plane to do so. It is the energy plane in which the formless becomes the formed. It is a mixed vibratory level and it contains, what you call in your context, good and evil. When you open yourself to lesser influences, you may be fooled into thinking that what you are receiving is of a higher nature because the personal, ego self can distort what you receive. You do not want to open yourself to guidance from lesser evolved beings or from your own ego self. You must always seek the highest counsel from the Creator through your Spiritual family. Therefore, do not seek communication from anything other than the Creator. Do not worship spiritual teachers, worship the Creator. Do not seek psychic phenomena, seek only the Peace of God. In this way, the messengers that are of the highest assistance will come forth. Your motive will affect your ability to draw on higher influences and avoid lesser ones. Thus, you must keep your motives clear and pure. Seek first the Creator and all you need will be provided.

"In my Father's house are many rooms. If it were not so, would I have told you that I go to prepare a place for you?" (John 14:2)

The Teachers Speak

Your life is a

Spiritual Journey.

Lesson 3 - Life as a School

The Teachers Speak

Lesson 3

Life as a School

We will speak to you this day about your life as a spiritual journey. The true reality about your life is that your life is a school. You enter this school just barely able to see that there is something beyond that which you see with your physical eyes. This glimpse is enough, however, to keep you seeking more of the light of the Creator. The lessons you are to learn in this school are an intricate part of your everyday life. They are the fabric from which your life is woven. You will begin to understand that all your life experiences are designed to teach you. Each experience gives you the opportunity to choose an awakened path or a path of ignorance. When choosing ignorance, you are choosing to ignore that which is already known at a deeper level of your being. At every juncture you have an opportunity to call forth the higher energies of the Creator or wallow in the human viewpoint where there is pain and suffering. A glimpse of a higher spiritual reality will lead you to the understanding that your life is not finite, as is believed by the majority of individuals in your world. Your life is a process of spiritual unfoldment in which your true self awakens to that which already exists.

You may feel that when you die, you sleep.
However, while you are alive, you sleep.

The sleep through which you move through life causes you many difficulties and much suffering. When you awaken from a night's rest, the sleepy feeling leaves you in waves like layers. As you enter the conscious spiritual journey, it is like one layer of sleep being lifted at a time. Such layers of consciousness are experienced as many veils, one veil in front of the other. You strain to see greater light yet, the veils dim your view. As you begin to understand that the purpose of your life is a process of allowing the veils between worlds to lift, you will be more content with your life as earthly accomplishments become less important to you. In this way, the grace of the Creator brings you to your curriculum.

Your individual and unique curriculum begins by choosing the circumstances of your birth in each incarnation. This you do not do alone but with the assistance of souls of greater evolutionary understanding. Together you fashion a life of probabilities that can bring you the lessons you need to progress spiritually. When choosing the life circumstances of your next incarnation, you are focused on moving, as quickly and efficiently as possible, in your spiritual evolution. You are not concerned about the pain these chosen circumstances might cause you once you are incarnated. You observe other individuals dealing with extreme life circumstances and wonder, "Why would anyone choose to enter into an incarnation with such conditions?" It is important to remember that each soul's life choices are based on their next step for spiritual evolution. You cannot understand, nor should you judge, the purpose of a life lesson of another. Only the individual can truly understand the purpose of a particular incarnational choice.

Before incarnation, you choose your
point of entry into a body vehicle.

You choose the souls through which you will be born, your race, sex, location and time of entry which set the stage for your incarnation. All of these factors create probabilities to encounter the experiences that will advance your spiritual evolution. For example, if one chooses to incarnate in a location of great poverty, it is probable that they will experience great poverty. This is not a punishment by the Creator, it is a choice made by an evolving soul to place itself in a context in which it will learn lessons that only such a context can provide.

Those who bring forth your body vehicle have a great deal to do with setting the stage for life lessons. For the most part, a soul is drawn to be a part of a family unit in which previous associations have occurred. Family relationships are a most important aspect of the school of life. Family relationships are often intense and can endure over the length of an entire incarnation thus allowing ample time for spiritual lessons to be learned by all in the family unit. Your lives are not predetermined in the sense that specific occurrences are destined to manifest. Your life, as it has been created by you, offers you the opportunity to grow spiritually. If you take advantage of these opportunities your lessons will become less severe. In other words, if you are willing to apply your highest spiritual understanding to a situation that presents itself to you, the severity of such a challenge will be diminished and your curriculum will become more subtle. This is the natural progression of the spiritual journey.

It is most important to understand that your life is your spiritual journey and the spiritual journey is your life. Do not place undue focus on the content of your life, on your possessions and on your accomplishments in the world. If you do, you will miss the true gift of life itself. Do not waste your time and energy comparing your life to the lives of others. Each life is a spiritual journey, a gift of grace by the Creator. Do not judge your experiences or those of others as good or bad. You may experience them as painful or joyous, however, do not cast any of them away from you. Embrace them as an opportunity to practice seeing the greater light of the Creator in all things thus bringing you one step farther in your spiritual evolution. You may think that highly spiritually evolved individuals will have a less challenging life experience. This is the world's faulty logic. Those of greater spiritual evolution may live lives of great challenge. However, their challenges will be in proportion to their ability to bring the grace of the Creator into seemingly overwhelming circumstances.

You cannot know the true reason for another soul's choices.

Therefore, stay focused on your own path. Some life experiences give you a greater opportunity to advance spiritually than others. Experiences given by the grace of the Creator for the greatest spiritual advancement will be those you cannot avoid or reconcile with your intellect. They will seem inexplicable to you. These experiences simply appear and their appearance is usually perceived by the ego self as some form of injustice or punishment. When you view such an experience from your true self, you will understand that, even if painful, the experience is an opportunity to see the light of the Creator at work. Always remember that the Covenant of Peace is with you and that you can never be outside of unconditional love. This is an unshakeable truth whether you believe it to be or not. When you bring this truth into your conscious awareness, it transforms every experience into an opportunity for greater spiritual growth.

Experiences that give you the greatest challenge bless you with the greatest spiritual advancement. Such growth experiences often have a theme throughout an individual's lifetime. Thus, a type of experience will repeat itself in different ways and at various times throughout the individual's incarnation. Each time it presents itself, the opportunity for advancement is given. As an individual advances, a recognition of a theme may emerge. When this occurs, the next time such an opportunity arises, it will be with greater clarity and less suffering. As you advance, clarity will continue to grow and suffering will continue to diminish. This is because with greater light comes a greater willingness to release the human tendency to judge, separate and blame, which perpetuates suffering. When this occurs you will enter into a greater peace with who you are, where you come from and where you are going. You become content with the understanding that your life is a process of spiritual evolution rather than a race of acquisition. You will be thankful for such insight and begin to flow through your life's curriculum with greater ease, greater faith and a greater understanding of the wondrous love of the Creator, ever drawing you toward itself.

Your life in the body has two purposes. The first purpose is spiritual evolution. The second purpose is more individual. Within each incarnation, agreements have been made to assist others before entering the body vehicle. These are agreements of service. For most, there are several of these agreements, many of which are fulfilled through daily life with those with whom they live, such as family members. As individuals evolve through various incarnations and become more spiritually aware, their individual purpose becomes more defined. Their service agreements will be with a wider audience and their individual purpose will become more specific.

A specific role cannot be discovered by the intellect as the ego self may distort the importance of your assignment. Your intellect will either overestimate or underestimate your role. The only way to determine a specific purpose is to focus on your life curriculum and allow the teaching aspect of your mission to emerge through meditation and by awakened choices you make in your daily life. Therefore, do not seek to know what your individual purpose may be outside of your commitment to spiritual evolution. Focus on spiritual growth and the more specific service you are designed to express will emerge naturally. You must humble the ego aspect of your being to understand what light you have to share. As the veils begin to lift and the light of the Creator begins to awaken you to a greater degree, you will know what form your service must take in the world.

"For everything there is a season, and a time for every purpose under heaven." (Ecclesiastes 3:1)

The Teachers Speak

I am not

at war with

the world.

Lesson 4 - The Earth

The Teachers Speak

Lesson 4
The Earth

I am not at war with the world;
I am not at war with myself;
I am not at war with God;
I am not at war with
my brothers and sisters.
There are no enemies.

We will speak to you this day about the nature and purpose of the earth. Many of you have a great concern for the welfare of planet earth. There is a growing recognition that the earth is vulnerable to misuse by its inhabitants. This distresses you as you begin to understand that it is the earth that sustains your life in the body. It is the earth that gives you an opportunity to reclaim your spiritual heritage.

The earth is an organism, a living thing, as you are a living thing. Some believe that the earth and all visible forms are illusions. Others believe that the earth and all visible forms are the only reality. Both of these viewpoints are incorrect. Your planet is neither illusion nor the only reality. If it were entirely illusion there would be no need for its existence. From our perspective, the earth is what you might describe as a hologram, a projection of consciousness. This projection is held in existence by souls who are assigned to keep its basic structure in place. These beings are throughout creation. They are assigned to hold the many physical universes intact through their consciousness. This may seem strange to you and you might be concerned that such celestial beings will have a lapse in focus. We assure you that such assignments are only given to those groups of entities who are evolved enough to fulfill their assignment without faltering. Thus, your planet is continuously generated through the celestial consciousness of evolved beings. Simultaneously, the earth is experienced as a physical reality while your Essence functions within a body vehicle. You must hold both viewpoints to correctly understand your planet. If you believe your planet is entirely an illusion, you will have no regard for its needs. If you believe the earth is just physical matter, you will have too great a concern.

Planet earth has a great capacity to regenerate, just as your body vehicle has the ability to heal. However, the regenerative powers of the planet and the body are not without limits. You can abuse your body beyond its capacity to sustain physical life. If you do, you will make your transition and your Essence will no longer be functioning within that particular body vehicle. This is true for planet earth, as well. Even though it is sustained through the focus of the celestial beings assigned to do so, it has limits within its physical manifestation. You cannot hold the earth in disregard and expect it to sustain your body vehicles. Your body vehicles depend on the elements of the planet to maintain life. Therefore, as temporary physical beings in a world of a temporary physical manifestation, you are linked and cannot be separated. If your physical world is destroyed, your ability to function within it will also be destroyed. The complete destruction of your planet would be difficult to accomplish, however, it can be damaged to the extent that it would no longer be able to sustain life. You might ask, "Why must I function within the confines and limitations of a body vehicle and a planet that is finite in its appearance?"

It is necessary for your Essence to
evolve through spheres of limitation.

A sphere of limitation reflects back to an Essence the level of God consciousness it has attained. Those of you on the earth have a level of understanding that is comparable to the level of limitation you experience on the earth. You may feel that you experience a great deal of limitation within the context of the earth and your body vehicles. However, universes exist in which there are even greater limitations, some in which the inhabitants do not even have freedom of movement.

Their environment reflects their consciousness. There is no judgment. This is simply a necessary out-picturing of the consciousness of the souls in these realms.

Your earth can be destroyed to the extent that it will no longer sustain body vehicles. This has happened in other realms. The Essences who were originally assigned to evolve through them have been placed in other contexts. You have among you individuals who were originally assigned to another world for their spiritual evolution. These individuals are both more advanced and less advanced than you. Those placed on earth who are less evolved will find the freedom you enjoy frightening. They may have a difficult time functioning within your context. Those of a more advanced consciousness will find it challenging to live within the limitations of the earth and physical body. However, the majority of souls on your planet are evolving within their original assignment. If you destroy the earth to the point at which it can no longer sustain life in the body, you will be assigned to another world through which to evolve.

How can a planet be destroyed when it is held in place by beings assigned to do so? These beings have very specific assignments. Their assignment is to continuously envision the earth in its original state of creation. They continue to do so as this is their service. However, they cannot control what humanity does to the planet once placed within its context. It is up to the collective will of those on earth to safeguard its ability to sustain life.

*Degrading and polluting your environment
is a form of mass suicide.*

It is the result of individuals who do not yet understand their true nature. There are individuals on the earth whose primary focus is remaining in the body vehicle for as long as possible. We call these souls, "keepers of the earth." They are evolving; however, they are at a stage in their evolution in which their function is to care for the planet. They are actively engaged in maintaining the life-sustaining nature of the planet. They perform a great service by maintaining the planet in a habitable state. Your planet is a very important school. It is a place for growing, evolving and rediscovering your true nature as offspring of the Creator.

Would you build a school and then deliberately destroy its foundation? You would not! You must think of your planet in this way. You must not destroy the earth's ability to sustain your life but use it as a classroom, a place from which to graduate and move onward. When you graduate from this world you move on to another sphere. It will also have limitations and an environment uniquely designed for spiritual growth. Most individuals incarnate within their planet of origin many times before graduating to the next level of more expansive parameters. Do not be concerned about the number of incarnations it may take you to graduate from planet earth! It is not a race, but a process of unfoldment.

How do you preserve your planet and your body vehicles? You do so by recognizing their needs and by attending to those needs. This is not complex. It is a matter of understanding the value, even though temporary, of your physical context. You must attend to your planet, you must save its water, forests, and atmosphere. The earth can be perfectly balanced when it is properly cared for. The earth has the ability to rebalance itself, however, you must stop wounding it. When you do so, you wound yourselves. Some may think, "I am worthless, my time on earth is of no consequence so I will indulge my senses to the fullest! I do not take any responsibility to future generations who have need of this planet." When you abuse your planet, you reveal that you do not have an understanding of your spiritual nature. You are not dust in the wind! You are a spark of divine light which has taken form and is being ever drawn to the all-encompassing love of the Creator.

You must see yourself as magnificent. You must see your planet as an out-picturing of this magnificence. As you do, you will feel empathy and gratitude for your body and your planet. Begin with the recognition that you are an important part of God's plan. We do not say this to enhance your ego. Your ego will decrease as you grow spiritually and completely dissolve when you move out of your physical body. Your ego is a temporary construct, created to help you function in the body vehicle. Thus, you must recognize the magnificence of your "beingness" without involving the ego. As you do, you will begin to recognize the significance of your planet and you will desire to become actively involved in maintaining its ability to sustain life.

The ego self only considers its immediate wants and needs. When it goes unredeemed, it will fulfill its desires without regard for the damage it might cause to the environment and others. Think in terms of future generations with the understanding that you may be among one of those future generations when you return to a body vehicle! You must put aside personal desires and immediate gratification for the preservation of your world. Celestial beings cannot save you from yourselves. We can, however, open you to a greater experience of the divine light of which you are made.

"God said, "Let us make man in our image, after our likeness; and let them have dominion…over all the earth." (Genesis 1:26)

The Teachers Speak

Who you truly are

cannot die or

be destroyed.

Lesson 5 - The Body Vehicle

The Teachers Speak

Lesson 5

The Body Vehicle

We will speak to you this day about the body vehicle. Each individual in your world is an offspring of the Creator. You are an eternal Essence that never dies but evolves and joins with others in the recognition that you are already one with the Creator. Your Essence is your unbroken link with the Creator. It is a thread of unconditional love, eternal peace and enduring wisdom. Your Essence is who you truly are. Your Essence has individuality and evolves in a greater context than your present physical incarnation. In other words, your Essence has been awakening through many experiences during many incarnations. As a human being you have selected the earth plane as your primary school for conscious spiritual evolution. Your incarnations appear to follow one another because you currently dwell in linear time. In truth, all experiences occur simultaneously. This concept is beyond your present capacity to grasp. We simply mention this to help you understand that your evolution is both continuous and complete at the same time. It is not important to grasp this while you are in a body vehicle. However, you must realize that your life is for the purpose of spiritual evolution and that you are eternal.

As you desire to consciously join with the Creator, the unbroken link with your source accelerates its magnetic pull and you enter into the spiritual journey in earnest. You have many incarnations of ignorance and darkness before awakening to your true nature. These incarnations are lived almost solely out of the fear-based, ego self. As a result, negative karma has been sown. Due to living in ignorance of your true self, you have transgressed the Golden Rule many times. You have victimized others and have been victimized by others. As you awaken, the healing of negative karma begins. Many of you are now emerging from this cycle in which you have primarily been involved in healing past karma. Your Essence is the aspect of you that knows that life is continuous, that your life has purpose and meaning and that knows you are greater than your own skin. Your Essence is the aspect of you that is capable of loving, capable of experiencing peace, capable of drawing upon the wisdom of the Creator to express in the world. Personality is born of your humanness that we call the ego self.

When your Essence is prepared to re-enter a body vehicle, it does so in an orderly manner. You may ask, "Where am I when in between incarnations?" You are home, a vibrational dwelling plane of light. A school of physicality, such as the earth, is a very intense experience. In between incarnations, your Essence returns to its Spiritual Family. Each of you has a vibration that is of a particular Spiritual Family. All Spiritual Families are born of the Creator and will eventually be joined as one. The vibrations of the Spiritual Families are different; however, no family vibration is better or less than any other. Thus, when the physical vehicle is no longer capable of maintaining a dwelling for your Essence, you return to your Spiritual Family. During this experience you are assisted in reviewing and assimilating what you have learned from your previous incarnation.

Judgment Day does not occur as envisioned by your religions.

There is no judgment when you are home with your Spiritual Family. There is, however, assessment. Essences with greater understanding help ones of lesser knowledge review their previous incarnation. This is done in an objective manner, without emotion or fear. Its purpose is to help you understand the progress you have made and the areas in which you need further experience to progress. The purpose of this assessment is to assist you in setting up the circumstances of your next earthly experience. Also, you must rest in between incarnations. The earth is a most intensive school! Therefore, your Essence takes a needed respite in between incarnations. Your Essence does grow and evolve while in between incarnations, however, the greatest periods of spiritual growth occur when you are in a body vehicle.

Your current science has deemed the physical body to be like a machine which it tries to fix when it is not functioning properly. However, the body vehicle is multidimensional and is comprised of several vibrational levels. These levels must be considered when seeking to heal the body when it is out of balance. In your context, individuals have a mental body, an emotional body, an energy body as well as a physical body. These four bodies correspond to the four-dimensional world you are evolving through at this time. When your Essence enters into a physical incarnation, it must move through the astral plane which forms matter. The purpose of the astral plane is to transform higher energies into physical level vibrations. Physical energy vibrations are much slower and denser than are Essence vibrations. Therefore, when an Essence enters into the denser vibration of a physical body, it must do so in a manner that enables it to be housed in the earth vibration.

The thought processes of an Essence create the mental, emotional and physical bodies. When an Essence is in between incarnations, it chooses its next incarnation in terms of vibration and form. For example, an Essence chooses whether the next incarnation will be experienced as a male or female, as heterosexual or homosexual. It chooses race, economic status, location and time of entry. When possible, an Essence chooses the individuals through which their body vehicle will come forth. All of these choices are made to set up optimum circumstances for spiritual growth. If negative karma needs to be healed, an Essence may be drawn to particular individuals through which it desires to come forth. All of the factors involved in the reincarnation process are very complex.

When you are in your pure Essence form,
you choose your next life circumstances with clarity
and with the assistance of your Spiritual Family.

You make these choices objectively, without emotion and without the memory of physical, mental, and emotional pain. You may ask, "Why would I choose to be incarnated at this time, in this place, through these individuals?" You have made these choices for a greater purpose, to enhance your spiritual evolution. These choices are made without considering the human pain and suffering they may create. When you are in your Essence form your only focus and concern is spiritual evolution. While in between incarnations, your choices are based solely upon what manifested circumstances will give you the greatest opportunity to grow.

An Essence must move through the astral plane to transform higher energies into matter. Your Essence holds in consciousness the parameters of the desired incarnation as it enters into the process of moving into a body vehicle. You may understand this as collecting the necessary equipment to function and survive in the physical realm. You must gather an emotional body and mental body as you enter into the physical body. Your intellectual capacity is determined by the conscious thoughts of your Essence as it gathers the mental body vibration. If it is to the advantage of an evolving Essence to be highly intelligent, then the mental vibration created will be one of high intelligence. If it is to the advantage of the evolving Essence to be of lower intelligence, then this will be the level of intelligence that will be gathered at the time of entry. This is also true of the emotional body. If it will be of service to the Essence to be highly emotional in the new incarnation, this will be the vibration the emotional body will gather at the time of incarnation. If it serves the purpose of the Essence to have an emotional body that is relatively calm and peaceful, this will be the level of vibration of the emotional body the Essence will gather through the astral plane. Of course, a physical body must be available to the Essence by the coming together of two individuals already in incarnation.

Many Essences, ready for incarnation, remain on the astral plane awaiting a body vehicle.

Those with strong karmic ties will be incarnated more quickly as the individuals already on the planet will feel an urgency to procreate. Those Essences entering incarnation with less karmic backlog will focus upon entering a body vehicle that best serves their spiritual purpose. Thus, a body vehicle may be chosen for various reasons in the same manner that the mental and emotional bodies are chosen.

Sometimes, this will mean that a strong, healthy body will be chosen. For other reasons, a body vehicle with health challenges to overcome will be chosen. Each incarnation and the choices that are made by the entering Essence are unique, having a specific purpose and expression. The whole process of entering into physical form is complex. The success of such a venture depends upon the ability of the Essence itself to remain focused and clear about its intended purpose. Essences of greater spiritual evolution are capable of greater focus. Therefore, as you awaken, grow and evolve, your incarnations will become more specifically geared to your ultimate purpose of conscious joining with the Creator.

Once incarnated, you may not remember your spiritual home or previous incarnations. Some Essences do not recognize or readily accept the body vehicle. An Essence may not bond with the physical vehicle for some time. Those drawn to earth quickly, with an urgency to heal karma, will enter the body vehicle early in the process of its formation in the womb. Essences of a more evolved nature may enter the physical vehicle more reluctantly. Such an Essence may be less than fully engaged in their body vehicle throughout their incarnation. The challenge in every incarnation is to remember who you truly are, an eternal being housed in a temporary physical vehicle. All Essences, whatever their level of remembrance, must learn to function within the dense vibration of the physical world. For some there is little adjustment. For others, the task requires a great deal of focus and concentration. However, every incarnated Essence must accept physical life as a gift from the Creator designed to enhance and accelerate their spiritual evolution.

Your life must be used for its intended purpose rather than wasted on addiction and distraction.

Each Essence must understand that the health of their emotional, mental and physical bodies is important to supporting their spiritual evolution. The mental, emotional and physical bodies are linked.

They cannot be separated. You cannot treat a mental imbalance without affecting the emotional and physical aspects of an individual. You cannot treat a physical imbalance without affecting the mental and emotional balance of an individual. This is the basis for holistic healing. Mental, emotional and physical bodies are comprised of energy vibrations. When you understand that they are a whole unit, directed by your Essence, you will understand where true healing lies. If an individual is out of balance within their Essence, their other bodies will be out of balance as well. You can patch up the body and keep it running, you can temporarily calm the emotions, you can bring insight into the mind, however, this is not true healing. To maintain balance in the total organism there must be recognition that your true self, your Essence, is eternally connected to the Creator. All vibrations throughout the universe emanate from the Creator. The Essence transforms and heals because it brings into balance all of the vibrational levels of the manifest physical vehicle. The body must be respected and maintained on the level of its existence on the earth. The body must be given proper fuel and movement, this is what is required. Beauty, as adornment, is not necessary. True beauty is the Essence fully expressing through the body vehicle. You need not be concerned with worldly standards of beauty. Your focus must be on the health of the body as your Essence cannot fulfill its purpose in the world unless the body vehicle maintains its balance and ability to sustain life. Your body must always serve the purpose of your Essence, your spiritual growth.

"In the beginning was the Word, and the Word was with God, and the Word was God...all things were made through him and without him was nothing made that was made." (John 1:1-3)

*I am not at
war with
my brothers
and sisters.*

Lesson 6 - Relationships

The Teachers Speak

Lesson 6

Relationships

We will speak to you this day about your relationships with one another. There are those who believe that to reach union with the Creator they must separate themselves from the world, spending all of their time in contemplation and meditation. Those who are suited to such a life are few and they are fulfilling their purpose by working in this solitary manner. For the vast majority of individuals, the spiritual journey is blessed with many relationships. While your Essence is housed in a physical body, you appear separate from one another. From the viewpoint of the fear-based, ego self, you are separate. This perspective carries with it a fear of being harmed by the "other" and a need to compete for survival based on the belief that resources are finite. This belief in separation creates the victim/victimizer drama.

The play of victim/victimizer begins on an unseen energy level. An individual who perceives themselves to be a victim will emanate an energy that is recognized by an individual who seeks to victimize. The energy of the victim draws the energy of the victimizer and the individuals come together to begin the play. Both the victim and the victimizer are functioning out of their personal, ego self which believes that it is separate from all others. The victim and victimizer will continue to play their parts until one individual in the scenario awakens and chooses to no longer participate. Because it is the energy of the victim that draws the victimizer, it is most often the awakening of the victim that begins to change the drama. Most people sympathize with the victim and despise the victimizer. However, both roles in the drama stem from the same ignorance as both individuals have not yet seen the light of the Creator within themselves. The victim and victimizer scenario can be karmic in nature. Individuals may be drawn to one another to complete a pattern that began in a previous incarnation. However, this is not always the case. If the energy of a victimizer is looking for a victim with whom they have had no previous association, they will find one. If a victim is looking for a victimizer with whom they have had no previous association, they will find one. Thus, a new karmic drama begins that may carry over into future incarnations.

The victim has a greater motivation for awakening to their true nature than does the victimizer as the victim generally endures more pain and suffering. However, the victimizer is also suffering. A victimizer projects their anger and fear onto the victim which can make it difficult for them to recognize what is truly occurring in the relationship. It is not impossible for a victimizer to awaken to their true spiritual nature. The grace of the Creator can come forth and express through each of them at any moment. When the victim or victimizer awakens to the truth of who they are and that they are one with each other, the process of healing past, present and future karma begins. Healing may progress slowly, however, it cannot be impeded once it has begun.

You have all been both victims and victimizers.

It is important to understand this link in your relationships as you are called to evolve past such scenarios to recognize complete oneness with your brothers and sisters. If you view one another from the perspective of your higher selves, you will no longer victimize or allow yourself to be victimized. When you understand your true nature as an eternal offspring of the Creator, you will begin to recognize that the divine nature in you is the true nature of all others. Without this understanding, the victimizer will inflate their own importance while the victim continues to deflate their importance.

The true purpose of relationships in your world is to equalize and then join. Joining is accomplished through the recognition of the divinity in all persons as they express through human form. As long as an individual is functioning as a victimizer they cannot recognize or accept their divine self. The same is true for the victim. When you find yourself in a situation in which you are either playing a victim or victimizer, you must choose to stop the role you are playing by stepping outside of your current thoughts and emotions. Calling upon the grace of the Creator will allow you to see the other person as yourself. God's grace is an ever-present gift that will show you the truth that when you victimize another, you are literally victimizing yourself. For the grace of the Creator to work to heal such a relationship, a choice must be made. The victim must choose to no longer be victimized and the victimizer must choose to no longer victimize. If just one of these individuals makes this choice, the dynamic between them will change and healing will begin.

The emotional and mental bodies are unseen aspects of your physical being. When your Essence enters into the physical realm, it collects the necessary energy bodies designed to help you navigate in the physical world. Therefore, it is necessary for you to have a mental, emotional and physical body within the earth context. The emotional body enables you to connect with your environment and with one another on an experiential level. The mental body manifests as the intellect which allows you to engage the world of form with reason and to place your life experiences in a linear format. Your body vehicle gives you the means through which to express the mental and emotional aspects of your being. When an individual is engaged in a victim/victimizer drama, the mental and emotional bodies are in charge. These two aspects can work together to enhance an individual's awareness of their true self or they can be used to trap them within the ego self.

Negative thoughts feed negative emotions.
Negative emotions feed more negative thoughts.

This cyclical pattern will escalate if not consciously broken. Thus, a victim/victimizer scenario may be broken by one person who ceases to generate the negative thoughts and feelings that hold the relationship in place. The victim/victimizer drama cannot continue unless each individual plays their part. For example, when a victim realizes that they have a choice to no longer be a victim, their emotional and mental energy will no longer broadcast the message, "I am a victim, come victimize me!"

Each individual must recognize the role they choose to play and make a choice to change that role. The energy of the victim or victimizer is self-generated. The choice to no longer be a victim or victimizer begins in an individual's thoughts. Thus, it is within the mental body that one begins to see the role they are playing.

The emotional body will seek to perpetuate this pattern. However, with persistent change in thought there will be positive change in the emotions as well. An individual wishing to step out of a victim or victimizer role must use their thoughts and emotions to claim and affirm their true identity as the beloved offspring of the Creator. They must also affirm the divinity of the other person before it can be seen to express through them.

Such recognition of divinity within the self and the other is not accomplished by a change of thought and emotion alone but also by one's intuitive faculty. The intuitive faculty is neither intellect or emotion, it is direct knowing from one's true self. Your true self, your Essence, does not reason or debate, nor does it know anger, fear or resentment. It simply knows itself. The intuitive faculty is the aspect of the Essence that translates into guidance that can be used in everyday life. When a victim or victimizer withdraws from their role and disengages from the destructive mental and emotional pattern they have created, they will then experience the intuitive faculty within themselves.

*When allowed to do so, the intuitive faculty
simply exists and works without difficulty.*

It is by the guidance of the intuitive aspect of your being that you will know what you need to do or stop doing in a victim/victimizer relationship. The choice to no longer be a victim or victimizer opens the door for the Creator's higher guidance as to how best to disengage from the destructive drama. Sometimes, higher guidance may be to stay within the proximity of the other and work together to heal the relationship. Or, one's guidance may be to physically remove oneself from the relationship and work to heal it from a distance. It may take time for such relationships to heal, however, once the true self has been awakened within at least one of the individuals involved, the process of healing will continue unimpeded.

Relationships have everything to do with your spiritual evolution. You do not and cannot return to the Creator alone. It is impossible to do so. As you evolve, you join and your awareness of true oneness increases as apparent differences decrease. Those who try to go to the Creator alone are seeking to do so from their ego self. They try to use their personal will to propel their spiritual unfoldment. Just as the Creator's sacred Covenant of Peace cannot be broken, your link with one another cannot be broken. You must assist one another on the spiritual journey. The victim/victimizer scenario is an important part of this assistance. Thus, even though it creates difficulty and pain in the physical context, its purpose is to bring all beings into conscious oneness.

"You shall love the Lord your God will all your heart...soul...and mind. You shall love your neighbor as yourself" (Matt. 22:36-39)

I am not
  at war
     with myself.

Lesson 7 - Acceptance

The Teachers Speak

Lesson 7
Resistance & Acceptance

We will speak to you this day about the power of acceptance. As you face the lessons prepared for you by your unique spiritual curriculum, you do so with an attitude of resistance or acceptance. To move forward in spiritual evolution, you must accept all of life. No aspect of life can be rejected or resisted if you wish to progress spiritually. Most individuals in your world resist life rather than embrace it, however, all great spiritual teachers and leaders have fully accepted life as it is currently manifesting. When you resist life and its gifts, you create a gulf between your intention to grow and growth itself. This gulf is like a wide river between your desire to evolve and your capacity to evolve. This gulf is self-created and for many years, perhaps many incarnations, overcoming it becomes your spiritual curriculum. On the other side of the river of resistance lies the experiences you must encounter that are uniquely yours.

Resistance to life is the natural reaction of the fear-based, ego self. In most cultures, resistance is encouraged and reinforced by an "overcoming" mentality. The ego wishes to confront, conquer, and control the laws of nature, including the actions of other human beings. The fear-based, ego self does not look within for truth but looks outward. Thus, it requires you to manipulate the world for survival rather than accept the world and the support of the Creator to move through it.

The ego self requires perfection so it creates a mask for you to wear. It says, "My true self is unacceptable. I will create a mask of the perfect me to present to the world. The world will then reward me with acceptance and thus, survival." The ego self cannot see that the opposite is true. The reality is that only by living as one's true self can you experience acceptance and support in the world. Even though the world knows little of self-acceptance, it will embrace the individual who embodies and expresses it. Such an individual is a genuine person who is able to see through the masks of others to touch their true selves. The ego self is the least perfect aspect of your being, and yet, it tries to be perfect.

Perfectionism is a disease of self-resistance. The desire to be perfect creates a wall of separation which takes a great deal of focus and energy to maintain. The Creator does not require you to be perfect, but desires you to be perfected. You cannot perfect yourself from the most imperfect aspect of your being! You can only be perfected by accepting your life as a spiritual journey that will include struggle, pain, love, joy and peace. Do not strive to be perfect. Do not reject any aspect of your being. You cannot find fulfillment and peace when you are at war with yourself. The disease of perfectionism prevents you from experiencing your true self. Only self-acceptance can defeat perfectionism. You must affirm self-acceptance before you can experience it. As you claim your birthright as a beloved child of the Creator, you will begin to remove the layers of false personality you have created. This is a part of the spiritual journey that cannot be avoided. The mask you have created will be slowly worn away as you continue to surrender the ego self to the higher self. The process of surrendering the ego must be constant. It is like the flow of water as it continually runs over rock. Its persistent flow will slowly wear it away.

A persistent claim upon the true self to come forth
wears down the false self you have made.

This process requires that you risk expressing your genuine self in the world. Surrender is not giving one's power over to the world. Surrender is releasing the false power of the ego self to the real power of the true self. Surrender is an inner process that brings about self-acceptance.

It is human nature to have a reaction of resistance to an unexpected challenge in life. It is important, however, to understand that you must first overcome your resistance before you can effectively face the challenge. When resistance arises, you can either choose to strengthen it thereby holding it in place, or you can choose to accept it as a gift from the Creator designed to accelerate your spiritual growth. Resistance may express as denial, procrastination, self-righteousness, anger or willfulness. When the personal will generates resistance, it says, "I do not accept what is occurring; I will not recognize what is occurring; I will not deal with what is occurring. I am going to will the situation to be more to my liking!" The personal will believes that if it is strong and stubborn enough, it can change what it fears and does not understand.

Resistance must be recognized and named when it arises. Naming resistance gives you the power to dissolve it. Resistance must be recognized as an opportunity for transformation. For example, if an individual is faced with the challenge of a life-threatening illness, resistance may express as a strong intent to fight it. This attitude will be reinforced and applauded by many others. In truth, however, it is not resistance that can bring about healing but acceptance that will lead to healing. An attitude of acceptance will allow you to be open to the guidance of your true self with the understanding that the Creator is at work in every situation.

> *Resistance holds a manifestation in place.*
> *What you resist, persists!*

Whatever you resist or deny separates you from the Creator. Your individual spiritual journey is designed to bring you to an experience of inclusion rather than exclusion; of joining rather than separation; of oneness rather than duality. Therefore, to name your resistance is to begin to overcome it. Overcoming resistance will greatly accelerate your spiritual evolution. Without the fear and resistance of the ego self, you will move through your various life lessons with greater speed and ease because you will move through them from the perspective of your true self.

Every time you name your resistance you are choosing to overcome it. To overcome resistance, you must move into the higher aspect of your being, into your true self. To overcome resistance, you must move from the willfulness of the ego self to the willingness of the true self. Within the true self you have no fear; within the true self there is no separation from the Creator; within the true self you cannot be in conflict with others and the world. Within the true self you have the opportunity to move to acceptance knowing that you literally have "no thing" to fear. Moving into such a consciousness, even for a brief moment, is like turning on a flood light in a darkened room. Once the light is on, acceptance of life will follow. Within the true self, loving acceptance reigns.

Within loving acceptance, you are able to embrace all situations, both painful and joyous; within loving acceptance you are able to love all individuals, those who express good and those who express evil; within loving acceptance you will know the Creator as an ever-present grace that is always available to you. Practicing loving acceptance is an important part of your spiritual journey. It enables you to consistently move forward and allows each life lesson to be fully embraced as a gift from the Creator.

"Judge not, that you be not judged. For with the judgment, you pronounce you will be judged and the measure you give will be the measure you get." (Matt. 7:1-2)

*I return to the
'Presence' moment
and I am filled
with Peace.*

Lesson 8 - Overcoming Fear

The Teachers Speak

Lesson 8

Overcoming Fear

We will speak to you this day about how to overcome fear. Fear is tremendously prevalent in the earth plane as it is an energy generated by the beings currently residing in body vehicles. Fear is not an energy born of the Creator. It is an energy that is created and circulated as a result of mankind's ignorance of its true nature and purpose for being on the earth. When an Essence first comes into physical reality, it has a remembrance of its true origin and life purpose. As a child begins to grow, however, its focus turns to navigating the physical world and these remembrances, for the most part, are lost. There are many outer influences thrust upon the child as they start to explore the physical world and begin to form language. In an effort to keep children safe from physical harm, adults begin to instill in the child a fear-based reality. Fear is transferred to the child even though the child's natural instinct is to move through life with an innate sense of protection. The human child is taught early that there is a great deal to fear within the physical realm. Fear that is instilled in the maturing child is, most often, imaginary fear rather than necessary fear.

Necessary fear is instinctual and exists in the present moment.
Imaginary fear is the anticipation of harm in the future.

When an individual is in immediate danger, they will instinctively know how to remove themselves from the harmful situation. These instincts are a part of the human animal nature and are important in maintaining life in the body. Your body vehicles have indeed evolved from the animal kingdom. Your true self, your Essence, has been temporarily implanted. In this way, you have taken on a body vehicle that is appropriate in the context in which you are functioning at present. Therefore, instinctual fear is a part of your animal nature. If allowed to function uninhibited, it will preserve your life many times during the course of an incarnation.

Fears of the imagination are self-generated by the anticipation of harm in the future. The consequences of living out of fears of the imagination are costly as they lead to a constant state of anxiety. The consequences of continual fear-based anxiety are great on many levels of your being. Such anxiety negatively affects the emotional and mental bodies, as well as the functioning of the physical body. Thus, generating imaginary fear is counterproductive and can be devastating to your overall well-being. It is this fear that must be consciously overcome, not only because it harms the body vehicle but, most importantly, because it brings into manifestation that which you fear.

The fear you generate within your imagination is perceived as real by your personal, ego self. The ego self is part of the physical body, as it should be. However, when the ego aspect of an individual is dominant, then fear of its own demise generates anticipation of calamity. The ego lives in fear of its own annihilation as it is totally dependent on the body vehicle. This is the aspect of you that believes you are your body and once your body dies, you no longer exist. This is a false identity you have created. Most individuals have developed their false identity to a greater extent than they are aware of their true identity as an eternal offspring of the Creator. The majority of individuals on the earth live out of the ego aspect of their being and are in constant fear for their very survival. Imaginary fear is generated from the belief that you are your body, that you are your mind, that you are your emotions. We tell you that you have a body, you have a mind, you have emotions and that you are none of these finite things. You are Spirit. We call this aspect of the Creator within you, your Essence. Your Essence is your true self. Within your true self, you know, beyond a doubt, that you are an eternal being.

Within your Essence you cannot be afraid
as your true self does not comprehend fear.

You may ask, "How do I overcome fear when I am so identified with my ego self and with my body as myself?" It is impossible to do so while you are primarily focused within the personal self, the self your ego has created. The perceptions of the personal self are drastically different from the perceptions of the true self. To overcome fear, you must consciously move to the higher perspective of your true self.

The consequences of dwelling on your fears are great! The energy of fear creates a strong mental and emotional construct that will physically manifest that which you fear. Your fears will be manifested as a result of the strong energy that fearful thoughts and emotions generate. The situation that you fear, in some form, will be drawn to you and will be placed directly in your path. The Law of Manifestation which states that persistent thought plus strong emotion equals manifestation, is always operating. Unless you cultivate a relationship with your true self, you will become engulfed by the manifestations of your own imaginary fear.

Manifestations created by imaginary fear generate greater fear resulting in more fear-filled manifestations. Thus, you will find yourself in a continual cycle of anxiety and its consequences. However, you do not have to remain entangled in this destructive cycle. The only way to break free from this cycle is to consciously cultivate an awareness of your true self, through spiritual practices such as contemplation and meditation. Many individuals do not seek a higher perspective until they are faced with a crisis. Reaching a low point in your life can inspire you to seek a more peaceful and harmonious way to live, one with less turmoil and pain. A crisis may be an illness, a heart-breaking relationship, a financial downturn or a deep disillusionment with life itself. Whatever it may be, a crisis is helpful when used to motivate you to seek a greater understanding of your true nature. This is a process of exhausting the limited capacities of the intellect, emotions and imagination to bring forth a sense of peace and well-being.

To overcome fear, you must reject the dominance of the fear-based ego and move into a greater realization and cultivation of your true self, the aspect of you directly linked to the Creator. To do so, you must choose to seek a more enlightened way of approaching life. As you begin your journey out of imaginary fear, your sincere desire to do so will assist you in coming into conscious contact with the self that knows that it is the springing forth of the Creator into form and expression. A strong desire to make this shift in consciousness is the impetus for your spiritual journey. However, the dominate fear-based self will strongly fight your attempts to move to a higher level of spiritual realization. Thus, you may feel you are engaged in a battle. Perseverance is necessary to win this battle. Your ego self must be assured that you are not trying to destroy it and that it is needed to help you navigate in the physical world. You cannot dispel fear from its own level. You must raise up your focus and allow it to fall away from neglect. Fear will die of its own accord when it is not fed by the negative imagination. It will die of its own accord when it is not energized by fear-based thoughts and emotions.

Anxiety is born of mental and emotional projections from the past into the future, totally bypassing the present moment.

The present moment is the "presence" moment, the only moment in which you can truly be in the presence of the Creator to experience the Peace of God. You are all heavily influenced by the collective fear consciousness of the human race. It is easier for you to live in fear of the future than to live in the peace of the present moment. This is why practicing some form of meditation is important as it is an attempt to return to the present moment. When you do so, even for an instant, fear will be released and you will become suspended in the light and love of the Creator...in the knowingness that you are one with all creation. In the "presence" moment your fears are dissolved. During such moments, your mental and emotional bodies are eased and your body vehicle is restored to its natural balanced state. You can practice "presence" moments during the course of your day by recognizing and releasing fear thoughts and emotions when they arise within you. To do so, stop, take a deep breath and affirm: "I return to the Presence moment and I am filled with peace."

"Therefore, I tell you do not be anxious about your life. But seek first his kingdom and his righteousness…" (Matt. 6:25 & 33)

There are no enemies.

Lesson 9 - Forgiveness

Lesson 9
Forgiveness

We will speak to you this day about the power of forgiveness. Forgiveness is the ability to transcend the illusion of separation between you and another. Within the forgiveness process, many awakenings occur. We wish to emphasize that forgiveness is a process rather than that which is accomplished instantaneously. The results of your actions become your karma. The consequences of your interactions with others manifests as your life experience. Karma, whether positive or negative, is the reaping of what you have sown in thought, word and deed. Future negative karma can be avoided before it manifests as its creation begins with thought that is then expressed in words and actions. Once action has taken place, you have sown the karmic seed and you will reap the harvest. There are individuals whose enlightened consciousness creates little or no negative karma. Most persons, however, continue to create future karma while dealing with the consequences of their past karma. As you learn to forgive, you heal past karma while evolving a more spiritually aware consciousness that creates less future negative karma.

Negative karma can be healed through the process of forgiveness. Both negative and positive karma are brought forth through the universal Law of Manifestation which states that thought plus feeling equals manifestation. In other words, what you dwell on in thought and enhance with feeling will manifest as your experience. Currently, you are experiencing what you have created in this incarnation and in previous incarnations. Your karma influences your entry into your body vehicle and will affect the circumstances of your birth. Do not assume, however, that those who are born into positive circumstances have less past karma to heal than others. This is not necessarily true.

Between incarnations, you make choices concerning your next experience in the physical body. These choices are made by your Essence with the assistance of higher beings assigned to help you.

The choices are made when in a consciousness that is totally focused on what you need most for continued spiritual evolution.

You might ask, "Why would an individual choose an incarnation in which they are abused, poor, sick or handicapped?" Incarnations of extreme suffering make no sense until you understand that these conditions have been chosen by the individual Essence to heal their karma. This is not punishment, it is opportunity. Your Essence knows that healing karma through forgiveness, surrender and love is the only way to evolve spiritually. You do not need to consult a psychic to remember your past karma. Your past karma is made manifest in the circumstances, challenges and relationships in your life right now. Therefore, a true forgiveness process is focused in the present moment. You may need to forgive someone in your past, however, if true forgiveness has not taken place in the relationship, the experience is still a part of your present consciousness. As such, it will continue to generate negative karma. The memory of previous incarnations has been dimmed by the grace of the Creator. It would not be wise for you to be flooded with the knowledge of all your past incarnations. This would overwhelm you and be counter-productive. Thus, we urge you to focus in the present to recognize the karma that needs to be healed.

Forgiveness is so important because it
heals past and future karma simultaneously.

All the mistakes you have made in the past and are making in the present are created out of fear and ignorance. Therefore, to become enlightened in your relationships you must strive to speak and act out of your highest understanding of love. It is important to understand that what you say and do to another person, you are literally doing to yourself because, in truth, you are one. If you cannot forgive someone out of love and compassion for them, perhaps you can forgive out of love and compassion for yourself! Whenever you interrupt the pattern of hurtful behavior with an enlightened thought followed by a loving action, you are erasing the negative consequences you were in the process of creating for yourself. It is never too late to forgive, it is never too late to heal and it is never too late to welcome the love and light of the Creator into a relationship. We do not ask you to forgive. We do not tell you to forgive. We bring to your awareness the absolute necessity to forgive.

You have each played the role of victim and victimizer throughout your many incarnations. The first step in the process of forgiveness is to acknowledge which role you are playing. An honest acknowledgment of your role begins the process. To acknowledge and accept responsibility for creating the situation gives you the freedom to change it. Once you are no longer the victim lost in pain and blame or the victimizer drowning in guilt and shame, you step into a higher consciousness. From a greater perspective you begin to see that the drama being played out in the relationship is a drama you have each agreed to play. You must take responsibility for your role in the relationship, whether the other individual chooses to do so or not.

This does not mean that you stop blaming the other person and begin blaming yourself! From a higher consciousness, you blame no one and thus, you become free to heal the karma between you. Taking responsibility for your role lifts you out of pain, blame, guilt and shame. As a victim, blaming the other individual is a position many people will support. However, you do not support yourself or the forgiveness process if you continue to blame the other. The victimizer, however, becomes stuck in a cycle of guilt and shame. When a victimizer takes responsibility, they are free to forgive themselves. Pain, blame, guilt and shame are like glue. If you remain in these states of consciousness, forgiveness cannot take place. Therefore, the first step is to acknowledge your role in the relationship. The second step is to take full responsibility for your role.

The third step is to open to the idea that, with God's grace, forgiveness is possible.

*This step requires opening to the
highest aspect of love within you.*

You cannot forgive yourself or others from the ego level of your being. The third step, therefore, requires surrendering your judgments, justifications, negative emotions and pain into the light of the Creator. To surrender lesser understanding for higher understanding you must be willing to place all pain, blame, guilt and shame on the altar to be sacrificed. You must be willing to release them, offering them up to be transformed into unconditional loving acceptance. Without your willingness to do so, forgiveness cannot occur. Therefore, your part is to be willing to let go, to let the grace of God accomplish the healing. You have to be willing to sacrifice the burdens of unforgiveness over and over again. Your willingness to do so may falter. You may be surrendered in one moment and in the next, take up your banner of pain, blame, guilt and shame once again. However, once you realize that the willingness to release these burdens is necessary in order to forgive and be forgiven, you will surrender them again and again until you are free. A heartfelt surrender and request for healing of a relationship will ultimately bring you the freedom and peace you truly desire. We do not ask you to condone hurtful behavior, we ask you to recognize the other as yourself. Whatever you have done to another, you have done to yourself. Whatever another has done to you, they have done to themselves. The healing process of forgiveness occurs within the true self, whether the other individual forgives you or not.

How will you know when forgiveness is accomplished?

You will know forgiveness has been accomplished when you experience a great release. You will know you have forgiven when you feel compassion and unconditional love for the other. You will know your karma is healed when you are at peace. You will know that forgiveness has taken place when you are overwhelmed by a sense of gratitude for the opportunity you have been given to step into the grace of the Creator. You will know that you have forgiven yourself when you feel free of guilt and shame.

You will know you have been forgiven when you feel a great love for yourself. In such a moment, you will experience unconditional love and oneness with the Creator and all creation.

"And forgive us our trespasses as we also forgive those who trespass against us." (Matt. 6:12)

The Teachers Speak

Oneness is within the duality you experience.

Lesson 10 - Good and Evil

The Teachers Speak

Lesson 10
Good and Evil

We will speak to you this day about good and evil. When contemplating good and evil, the question that must be answered is, "What is the purpose of duality in the world?" You use the terms good and evil to describe the human actions that result from those living in light or those living in darkness. Actions either produce more love, harmony and peace in the world or they produce their opposite: difficulty, fear and pain. Because this is true in your earthly experience, it is necessary to address the dual nature of your world. Many may ask, "If I am already one with the Creator, what am I doing here in a world of duality?" The purpose of such worlds as your own is evolutionary in terms of consciousness. You cannot consciously return to the Creator without moving through worlds of duality. When you are created you have no conscious awareness of yourself. To acquire a consciousness of self, you must move through various experiences that you would describe as being dark or light. You have within you an innate desire to return to your Creator in a fully conscious manner. This desire is implanted in your Essence from the moment of creation. Your consciousness is like an embryo that must develop and awaken to its true nature. As an embryo, there is little conscious awareness of self and no conscious awareness of your true nature or destiny. To recognize yourself, your Essence must enter worlds of both light and darkness. Where there is duality and contrast there is the ability to recognize the self. As you evolve, you begin to see that complete oneness is within all the duality you experience.

Your spiritual journey involves moving from unconsciousness to consciousness through recognition of what you are not! To do so, you must be in a context such as the earth where you presently reside. Contexts of duality are not ultimately negative or positive. Darkness is not negative; it is simply the opposite of light. For creation to occur, there must exist both negative and positive energy charges. You may believe that the solidity of your world is an illusion, however, while you are functioning within it, it is quite real.

Therefore, do not try to fly or walk through walls! The earth has a certain density and so does your body vehicle. You must function in three-dimensional reality because you are housed in a three-dimensional body. The purpose of entering a three-dimensional world is to gather experience. You gather experience much more readily within such a context because experiences are felt more strongly when in a body vehicle. You have strong mental and emotional bodies while in a physical body which allow you to have very vivid experiences that are then impressed upon your consciousness. You have experiences in this way that have profound effects on your journey toward conscious union with the Creator.

Within your present context, you have experiences you label positive or negative, good or bad.

However, it is not necessary to experience darkness to the degree that you do in order to understand the nature of the light. It is only necessary to experience darkness in order to help you recognize the light that is within you, the light that is you. You must understand that both darkness and light, negative and positive energies are neutral elements of creation. These energies are raw material you may use in a constructive or destructive manner, resulting in either good or evil manifestations in the world. In other words, you have a choice to use these neutral energies for the creation of good or evil. When you understand that the raw material for creation is neutral, you realize that the responsibility for good and evil in the world belongs to each one of you. Any individual who chooses to use the energy of creation in a destructive manner will, at some juncture, reap the consequences of such actions. This may not occur in their present incarnation; however, the consequences will be experienced, indeed. This is not a punishment by the Creator. The purpose of karma is to experience the other side of the coin, so to speak. In other words, if you victimize another individual, you will eventually experience what the victim experienced. It is only in this manner that you begin to understand, at a level beyond the intellect, that there is no separation between you and your neighbor.

In your reality, the illusion of separation between individuals is punctuated by the fact that you are temporarily housed in separate compartments. The truth is that you extend far beyond your skin.

Thus, the vibration of either darkness or light you project has a very wide sphere of influence. In your Scripture, it teaches that if you are angry with your neighbor, it is the same as if you are causing them bodily harm. Your consciousness is a powerful tool for either generating light or darkness in the world. With it, you create an atmosphere around you that draws like experiences to you. Whatever experiences you draw to you, whether you consider them negative or positive, they serve you when you understand that you are truly one with the Creator and all evolving souls.

I will give you an analogy. A coin is a three-dimensional object. It has two sides and a narrow center strip, its depth. Let us call the depth dimension between the two sides the neutral zone. From this neutral dimension, the coin can easily tip to one side or the other. Like the coin, there is an energy within you which allows you to experience both sides of creation, both darkness and light.

The more you experience darkness,
the more you will desire to live in light.

Many of you have experienced much darkness which has caused you to seek more light. Now, when you experience darkness, you can use it as an opportunity to become a generating station for greater light. Actions considered evil are generated by individuals who are so very cut off from the light within themselves that they become consumed by the darkness. Their existence is most painful to themselves and, of course, to those they victimize. There are reasons for such interactions. Do not try to determine what the reasons are. Do let the light of the Creator shine through you to guide your thoughts and actions as to how to uplift every dark situation you encounter.

When you project your own darkness onto others, you can begin to justify their destruction. This has occurred many times in your world and continues to occur in present time. Groups of people may become "scape goats" for the dark aspects of those who cannot accept their own human failings. This sets up a war between the forces of good and evil by those who believe themselves to be only good. Thus, those who believe themselves to be good seek to destroy those they believe to be evil. They do so while sincerely believing they are doing God's work. This, of course, is not God's work. It is the work of the human will, so separated from the loving acceptance of the Creator, that it justifies the torture and physical annihilation of others.

You are angry that there is so much injustice and suffering in your world as a belief in equality is fundamental in your reality. From the human perspective, all people should be created equal even though it is obvious that they are not. Human beings are not created equal in terms of physical strength, intellectual ability or life circumstances. However, it is true that all Essences that inhabit a body vehicle are created equal. Your life circumstances and your capacity to deal with them have been chosen by your Essence for the purpose of your spiritual evolution. You must view your life and the lives of others from this higher perspective to see the true purpose of your experiences on earth. You see people suffer with illnesses, poverty and abuse and you are naturally distressed. It is important to understand that just because an Essence has chosen a painful and difficult path for their spiritual growth does not mean that you stand by and watch them suffer with indifference. If your chosen path enables you to help alleviate their pain and suffering, you must do so. In other words, to fulfill your assignment, you must do what you can, right where you are, to support, defend and console those who are suffering. However, sometimes pain and suffering that cannot be alleviated may be chosen by an Essence for their spiritual evolution. The reason for such choices can only be known by that Essence when it no longer inhabits a body vehicle.

All lives are intertwined because you must grow and evolve together. Relationships offer the greatest lessons for spiritual growth in your context. In this way, you are each other's keepers. The journey to conscious oneness with the Creator begins with the realization of oneness with one another. How you interact with each other provides you with your most valuable lessons. Empathy, which is entering into the spirit of another person, is what is required.

Empathy joins, sympathy separates.

When you are empathetic, you acknowledge your oneness with the other. You may think that having sympathy for someone will bring you to feel oneness with them, however, the opposite is true. While sympathizing, you are looking at them from the outside with pity and, at the same time, giving thanks that you are not in their situation. No one should be pitied. Each Essence has chosen the path they are on for a higher purpose. You are, however, by virtue of your own purpose, required to be empathetic, to "walk a mile in their shoes" and to act to mitigate their suffering to the extent possible. This can only occur when your Essence fully recognizes that you are not separate from their Essence. Therefore, fully participate in the relationships in your life knowing that as you focus on the individuals placed on your path, you will see everyone as fellow spiritual travelers on the way to total conscious oneness with the Creator.

"You are the light of the world...Let your light so shine before men, that they may see your good works and give glory to your Father who is in heaven." (Matt. 5:14)

Those who teach,
must know.
Those who know,
must teach.

Lesson 11 - Spiritual Teachers

The Teachers Speak

Lesson 11
Spiritual Teachers

We will speak to you this day about spiritual teachers. There are many ways you receive assistance from spiritual teachers on your spiritual journey. The various levels of assistance come to you when you open to them by being willing to release your ego's control over your life. Releasing fear-based ego control requires focus and concentration. This is accomplished through meditation but also through daily, hourly and moment by moment monitoring of your thoughts and feelings. The practice of meditation builds a bridge between the self you believe yourself to be and your true self, that which is linked to the Creator through the Celestial System. It is not enough to build a bridge to your true self during meditation if you disassemble that bridge with thoughts of lack, limitation, fear and judgment throughout the day. All such thoughts and their accompanying emotions separate you from the Creator's presence. Thus, you must continue to build a bridge of communication between your ego self and your true self during the mundane activities of daily life. Meditation prepares you for entering your day in peace by establishing a connection with your true self. Ideally, you can then move through your life with this connection intact and approach each person and situation from your true self.

Your life is your spiritual journey's curriculum and thus, your best teacher. Every person and situation in your life teaches you by presenting you with a choice. The content of each encounter may be different; however, the choice is always the same. "Shall I respond from my fear-based, ego self or will I respond from my God-centered true self?" This choice is presented to you thousands of times each day. Your spiritual progress depends on how often you choose to confront your life lessons from the higher aspect of your being. This process can be assisted by the teachers of your Spiritual Family. True spiritual teachers are souls who have evolved to a greater level of understanding than your own. They are capable of helping you choose the "high road" in every situation. They do so by helping you step out of the turmoil generated by your personal, ego-based self.

Spiritual teachers may or may not express through the language of religion or spirituality. You can recognize them by observing how they express in the world. In your realm, there are many false teachers. Therefore, it is important that you are able to distinguish a false teacher from a true teacher. Use the following criteria: a true spiritual teacher will never claim to know all of God's truth or to be God; a true spiritual teacher will serve others without requiring adoration and praise; a true spiritual teacher will never seek to be worshipped; a true spiritual teacher will show the way but never claim to be the only way; a true spiritual teacher will not attempt to take away a student's life lessons but will assist them to use them for spiritual growth; a true spiritual teacher will live simply, their lives will be designed to support spiritual practice; true spiritual teachers will not lavish themselves with material possessions. If wealth should come to them, they will give it away to those in need. A true spiritual teacher will never take a student's power as they have no desire to exercise power over others.

The life of a true spiritual teacher will express peace and compassion in every thought, word and deed.

There are many in your world who proclaim themselves to be spiritual teachers. You must closely examine the teacher by observing their students, as students of the teacher are a reflection of the teacher. If students give their total allegiance to the teacher because they believe that the teacher is their only link to the Creator, beware. If students abandon their responsibilities in the world, especially to their off-spring, beware. If students desire to be rescued by the teacher and the teacher fosters this desire, beware. However, if students are being assisted to create a stronger relationship with the Creator, you may find that you are in the presence of a true spiritual teacher. A true spiritual teacher will have a vibration that is more refined than most individuals. Their spiritual vibration alone may be sufficient to teach and some teach only on this level. A true spiritual teacher may lead an ordinary life, and yet, their level of spiritual evolution will generate a vibration of loving acceptance that goes forth to assist others.

Some spiritual teachers are evolved beyond the need for physical incarnation. Such beings may teach through an individual whose spiritual development is sufficient to allow their teaching to come forth and express. Such out-of-body teachers work with an individual soul for many incarnations before coming through them. To discern a true out-of-body teacher from a presence of lesser vibratory evolution, apply the same criteria discussed to the channel and their students.

A concern for possible ego involvement is a constant dilemma for all spiritual teachers. For a teacher presently in a body vehicle or a channel for an out-of-body entity, the ego self must be kept in constant service to the true self. Some teachers who have attained a high level of spiritual understanding may fall from grace because they have given into the temptations of the ego, the temptation to use spiritual power for personal gain. Such an individual may begin to infuse their teachings with ego-driven, manipulative undertones. At first, it may be difficult for students to discern this shift in motivation. It will eventually, however, become apparent by observing the teacher's words and actions. Such a fall from grace can be devastating for the teacher and for the students. You may find that a spiritual teacher who truly assisted you in the past, has now become a false teacher. If this occurs, you must immediately release them with the understanding that Celestial assistance is always available.

Discerning the motives of a spiritual teacher
is the key to determining the purity of their message.

A true spiritual teacher's motivation will be to assist you in building your own bridge to the Creator, rather than to bind you to themselves, as if they are the bridge itself. Along your spiritual journey you will encounter both false and true teachers. Both will assist you. A false teacher will help you to develop discernment by reminding you that you must develop your own relationship with the Creator. The true spiritual teacher will assist you to build that relationship.

Do not stay with a false teacher once you realize that their motives have been compromised. Once you discern that the teacher has mixed motives and intentions, you must remove yourself. If you remain the disciple of a teacher with mixed motives, your spiritual progress will be delayed and you may be harmed.

Such harm will have to be healed before you can move forward once again. Therefore, take yourself out of harm's way immediately. If you stay you will no longer be learning discernment but you will be allowing yourself to be manipulated and victimized. This is not to your benefit nor to the benefit of the teacher as they must awaken to their own mixed motives to move forward. Most often such false teachers are not, what you would call, evil. They may have good intentions but lack sufficient spiritual understanding and should not be presenting themselves as a spiritual teacher. In a similar way, an individual who brings forth teachers, such as ourselves, must have pure motives and be spiritually prepared for true teaching to emerge. There are those who teach in this way who draw from available entities of lesser understanding. Thus, their teachings are of little practical use and may be harmful. Such unenlightened entities are seeking power in the physical realm and have found a willing voice through an individual with mixed motives. An individual who brings forth a true spiritual teaching from a non-physical realm must be one who seeks the Creator alone and does not desire to use such contact to manipulate and control others. A channel must have pure motives that can be discerned by observing their teachings and behavior. A true spiritual teacher, whether in the body or moving through a body, will always seek to assist their students to express from their true self.

> *A true spiritual teacher is a presence of*
> *loving acceptance and a beacon of peace.*

Do not be fooled by that which appeals to your ego. A teacher who deliberately enhances your ego is a false teacher. It is up to you to discern! It is up to you to purify your own motives so you may clearly see the motives of others. No teacher can take the spiritual journey for you. If one claims to do so, turn and walk away. Only you can place yourself on the spiritual path. Only you can keep yourself on the spiritual path. Your teachers, whether ordinary individuals in your daily life or spiritual presences of a higher vibration, are simply guide posts along the way. They are not the path itself, nor are they the destination.

"Beware of false prophets, who come to you in sheep's clothing but inwardly are ravenous wolves. You will know them by their fruits." (Matt. 7:15-16)

The Teachers Speak

The Teachers Speak

> *I am not*
> *at war*
> *with God.*

Lesson 12 - The Spiritual Journey

The Teachers Speak

Lesson 12
The Spiritual Journey

We will speak to you this day about the Spiritual Journey. To find your place in the Creator's vast plan, you must be willing to take the conscious spiritual journey. It is best to take the spiritual journey with the understanding that you are both ordinary and extraordinary. You are ordinary because you are but one of an infinite number of souls who take this journey. You are extraordinary because you have a purpose to fulfill within the plan that only you can accomplish. Once you awaken to the knowledge that you are an important part of the Creator's intricate tapestry of great beauty, you will ask yourself, "What is my soul's special thread and how is it woven into the cosmic design?" This question marks the beginning of your evolution toward conscious union with the Creator.

Embarking on the conscious spiritual journey will undoubtedly bring restlessness and confusion into your life as, to this point, you have been content to live according to the requirements of your environment and the values of your culture. To begin the conscious spiritual journey, you must be willing to step outside of the crowd, separate yourself from the masses and enter the process of individuation. This is not a process of ego enhancement in which the ego self seeks power and advantage over others. This individuation requires that each soul examine itself.

When the focus of your life turns to self-examination, you will begin to experience discontent, anxiety and inner conflict. Why? Because the contrast between what your ego desires to do and what your soul asks you to do, may be in opposition. The ego self perceives the process of individuation as antithetical to its safety and survival. To be safe, from the perspective of the ego self, you must remain fearful and ever vigilant, always perceiving yourself as separate from all others. The process of the conscious spiritual journey is one that leads to total inclusion, to the realization of complete oneness with all other souls and with the Creator. Entering this blissful state of oneness means death to the ego self which wants to avoid its own demise at all cost.

The inevitability of physical death brings you to the conscious spiritual journey. The fear of non-existence calls you to the necessary process of self-examination. If there were no end to your life in the body, there would be no spiritual evolution. It is the inevitability of death that prompts you to ask questions about the meaning of life, to ask if there is existence beyond physical death. Once you ask this question, you naturally begin to seek an answer. The answer lies hidden deep within your own soul. The fact that it is hidden is a great blessing. If it were easily known, you would make little evolutionary progress.

When you look at others you wonder what their life is like and you compare your life journey to their life journey. You make judgments, condemning or praising them, making them less or more than yourself. Judging and comparing yourself to others is harmful because it is a waste of your time! At the initial stage of awakening, your task is to focus on discovering the meaning and purpose of your own existence. Many unseen forces are operating in the lives of each soul. There is no advantage to condemning or praising others when you are ignorant of the unseen forces that influence their life and yours. Focus on your own awakening.

*Do not try to awaken others
when you are barely awake yourself.*

At a later stage in the spiritual journey, you will become a greater instrument of light for the Creator to use to help awaken others. At this early stage, your mission is to follow the glimpse of light you have seen so you may eventually awaken more fully.

True self-examination does not take place on the level of the ego self which will demand absolute perfection before acceptance can take place. Self-examination does not ask how good you are or how bad you are, it asks who and what you are. From spiritual levels of awareness, love is always flowing forth. You are continually bathed in an ocean of loving acceptance as this is the Creator's sacred covenant with all souls. Your true awakening is to open to the loving acceptance that is your true nature. Seek to know the answer to the question, "What is the meaning and purpose of my life?" When you do, you take the first step in the conscious spiritual journey. Do not be impatient to find the answer. The question is more important than the answer, for it is the question that will take you where you need to go.

The conscious spiritual journey must be taken whether you wish to do so or not. However, you do have a choice as to when to begin. We suggest that you lovingly release all resistance and enter into it willingly and joyously. Do not enter the spiritual journey with fear and trepidation. There are many myths concerning the nature of the Creator to which you are returning. Many of you would just as soon delay the journey because of these misconceptions. We cannot tell you of the Creator's full nature as it is a mystery to us as well. However, we can tell you that the mystery of the Creator must be entered into willingly. It is only by seeking God Experience that you will be at peace. An intellectualization of the spiritual journey is only helpful at its inception. The mind will be appeased, to some extent, by constructing expectations. Of course, the expectations of the mind will be faulty. The mind requires order thus, at the beginning of the journey, it is not detrimental to use your intellect to help you enter into the mystery of the Creator. God Experience is what you are truly seeking. It cannot be replaced by intellectual understanding.

God Experience comes to you by desiring it above all else! You must desire God Experience with all your being. However, you must not demand it. When you demand God Experience you do so from the personal aspect of your being. Thus, you are trying to enter into the mystery that is the Creator with the will of the ego. The ego assists you in physical life as it is necessary for your survival in the body. Thus, to have God Experience you must surrender your ego self. To enter the sanctuary of the true self, your personal, ego self must be temporarily set aside. Doing so may create fear as most individuals are overly identified with their ego self. If you believe you are finite and that you are only your mind and body, you will have difficulty moving into God Experience. To do so, affirm:

The Peace of God is all I seek, all I experience, and all I express.

To open the door to God Experience, you must be willing to release many things. The greatest of which is an over-identification with the self you have created. Your personal self is not your true self, it is the self you have constructed for survival in the world. It is the self you have created according to the specifications of your society, the time, locality and culture in which you live. The ego self carries a lot of excess baggage. You can visualize this as trying to move through a narrow gate carrying many pieces of bulky luggage. You will bump up against the framework of the gate and you will not be able to go through. In order to go through the gate to greater God Experience, you must be willing to "toss" some of your baggage.

What will convince you to release your baggage? What will convince you to do so is experiencing sufficient disappointment and disillusionment with the world and with the self you have created. Once you are truly tired of creating your reality from the imperfect level of your personal self, you will be quite eager to release your baggage. Most individuals cross this threshold in increments, throwing away their smallest bag first. Once you have had a glimpse of the love, light and peace of God you will be quite thirsty for more. Then, you must be willing to continue to release the baggage that is burdensome to you. This is the process of your spiritual journey while in a body vehicle. This process must be entered into with great desire, longing and surrender. Meditation is the journey's primary tool. However, you must not enter meditation while making demands of the Creator.

Meditation is a time to give as well as a time to receive. If you enter your spiritual practice in this way, you will find that you receive God Experience when you least expect it. You will receive when you have released all demands of the Creator. You may say, "If I am sitting in stillness and silence, what am I giving?" We will tell you what you are not giving! You are not giving more negative energy into the collective consciousness of your planet. You are transforming negative energy into positive energy which benefits the entire universe. Thus, you must enter meditation with a sense of giving rather than with demands to receive. Making personal demands during meditation will greatly frustrate your attempt at establishing a spiritual practice and may cause you to decide that it is not worth the effort. Therefore, carefully consider your attitude as you enter into spiritual practice.

You must be honest with yourself. Self honesty, without judgment or self-deprecation, is a necessary part of the spiritual journey. Without self honesty, you cannot accurately examine your motives. Other individuals can see your motives quite clearly. This may make you feel uncomfortable, however, it is true that individuals can be more objective when assessing the motives of someone else than their own. Along with practicing self honesty, it is essential to have an individual in your life who will honestly reflect back to you what they observe concerning your motives and actions. Most individuals enter the spiritual journey with mixed motives. Deep in their innermost being, every soul's true motive is to consciously join with the Creator. Often, there are many other motives layered upon this deep longing. Over time, these motives must be exposed and released if you wish to stay on the spiritual path. There are many ways to stray from the path. Some directions you take are simply detours and eventually will lead you back to where you started. However, some detours will take you into more and more self-deception. Once you are engulfed in self-deception, it can be difficult to extricate yourself. A sincere desire to have God Experience above all other things will instantaneously bring you back from the trap of self-deception. Part of self-deception is delusion. Your delusions may prevent you from the surrender and commitment necessary to bring you back to the spiritual path. Therefore, it is best to honestly check your motives every step along the way. Such a periodic assessment will, for the most part, keep you firmly on the path and you will avoid a great deal of difficulty and suffering.

Self-realization precedes God-realization. You must begin with yourself. If you truly seek God Experience, you will be given assignments to help you know yourself more fully. Remember, your life is your curriculum. The Creator is not sitting on a throne somewhere throwing you curve balls and tests! It is your life, as you move through it, that gives you the necessary lessons for your spiritual journey. It is your own great longing for God Experience that requires you to confront yourself, your motives, and your ego identity. Desire sets the process in motion. Continued desire and commitment to spiritual practice will guide you over and around any stones you may find on your path.

You are not alone. There exists a great energy of love that is drawing you homeward.

You would not be reading our words if you were not aware of the pull of the Creator within your own consciousness. This power is most extraordinary. It is with you to assist you every step of the way. It does not forsake you; it does not leave you desolate; it does not trick or test you. It simply draws you because you are its beloved offspring. We urge you to enter into the conscious spiritual journey with great joy, great love, surrender and a great commitment. Surrender and commitment will need to be renewed continually. This is understandable. You have not failed when surrender and recommitment become necessary once again.

Do not judge yourself but accept and love yourself. You are not to glorify your ego self nor diminish your spiritual self. You must embrace your entire self to move forward, to expand outward and upward. Accept the great gifts of the Creator as they come to you and become a channel of love and peace in the world. This is a most wondrous calling. It is time for each one of you to choose the spiritual journey' to choose it, embrace it, and enter into its mystery. There are many things that cannot be known or understood in your present state of consciousness. You will know, however, through God Experience, that there exists a glorious presence that is all wisdom, all love and abiding peace.

Prayer for the Spiritual Journey

Teachers of Peace

I awaken to the rhythm of love beyond measure
and joy beyond expectation. O'Blessed Spirit,
your grace now fills my every thought, word
and deed. I am blessed by the healing
power of your love. Help me to release
my fears and concerns. Free me from my
wants and desires. Find me fully open
and receptive to new life in your Peace.
Deliver me from my own creations
that I may behold Thy true creation
in its fullness and glory.

Amen

A Parable

The Spiritual Journey is like a woman who stands outside of a gate, peering longingly inside. As she looks through the bars of the gate, she sees a magnificent City of Light, a city that compares to no other she has ever seen. Its beauty draws her to enter the city. As she toils outside of the gate, she finally decides to follow her heart's desire and leave her familiar surroundings to enter the City of Light. She gathers her valuables together into bundles which she intends to take with her into the city. The first bundle holds her beliefs about herself, the belief that she is separate from all others and that she must defend herself against her enemies to survive. In the second bundle, she places her attachments. These include all of her worldly possessions but, more importantly, the loved ones she believes belong to her. In a third bundle, she gathers up her opinions and judgments about the world and the Creator. Carrying her many bundles, she arrives at the gate of the City of Light.

Out loud she declares her burning desire to enter the beautiful city and requests that the gate be opened to her. To her astonishment, the gate opens! With much anticipation, she tries to pass through the gate but finds that her bundles won't fit through. Determined to enter, the woman rearranges them, putting one on her head and the others under her arms. She tries again to enter but still cannot get through. After many attempts, she sits down in despair.

At that moment, she sees an old man standing at the gate. He has been watching her futile attempt to enter the city. He looks at her kindly and says, "You can't bring all of that burdensome baggage with you into the City of Light." She begins to explain to him why she needs all of this stuff. Suddenly, the man disappeared as quickly as he appeared. The woman then asks herself, "Am I willing to let go of some of this baggage to enter the beautiful city?" After struggling with this question, the answer she hears within her soul is, "Yes, I am!" She begins to rummage through her bundles examining each concept, belief, judgment and attachment. She decides that certain ones can be left behind but others she must certainly keep. Carrying somewhat smaller bundles, the woman makes another attempt to go through the gate into the City of Light. After some rearranging, she slips through the gate.

What a wonder of newness surrounds her! For some time, she is simply content to walk through the city experiencing its beauty and peace. Eventually, however, the woman becomes tired. The bundles she still carries have become increasingly heavy. She sits down to rest and when she looks up, she sees another gate! This one is even more magnificent than the first. The dazzling beauty she glimpses behind this new gate clearly can offer her an even greater peace.

Again, her desire to enter the second city opens the gate. Again, she tries to enter with all of her bundles. When she cannot get through the second gate, she realizes that it is because of the amount of baggage she still carries. She rummages through her bundles once again to see what else she can let go of. To her dismay, she admits to herself that she is unwilling to release more from her bundles at this time. Unable to get through the second gate, the woman decides to stay in the first City of Light, learning and growing right where she is. She is not in despair as before because she knows that one day, when she is ready, she will let go of more of her burdensome baggage. She knows that, when the time is right, she will pass through the second gate. There she will find a third gate, then a fourth gate, a fifth, a sixth, a seventh and beyond these, many more. The woman's perceptions are correct for she is now on the conscious spiritual journey. She has entered the process of self-examination with its inevitable unburdening and purification, given lovingly to her by the Creator. She knows that she must be present to this process and joyously accept the gifts of loving acceptance and peace she receives along the way.

Do not lay up for yourselves treasures on earth, where moth and rust consume and where thieves break in and steal...but lay up for yourselves treasures in heaven...for where your treasure is, there will your heart be also." (Matt. 6:22-23)

The Teachers Speak

We are pleased

to answer

your questions.

Lesson 13 - Questions & Answers

Lesson 13
Questions & Answers

After each lesson, the Teachers of Peace invited questions from the attendees. The following are selections from the question and answer periods.

On Forgiveness:

How do I let go of guilt and regret? Many of you are suffering from guilt and remorse. You must forgive yourselves for decisions you made when you were unable to make any other choice. In other words, forgive yourselves for not making better choices that you now see were possible to make. Regret keeps you in the past and guilt serves as punishment in the present. You must claim your birthright as a child of the Creator, not perfect but willing to be perfected as you experience life in a body vehicle. All life is energy emanating from the source of all life. It cannot be otherwise. As difficult as your present time on earth may be, it is best to reside in the present moment as much as possible. To release the past, affirm your true identity as an eternal child of the Creator. Do not let your ego self argue with this truth! This you will need to affirm daily, hourly, momently... a much better use of your time than dwelling in guilt and regret. When these negative thoughts and emotions arise tell them to "be gone" and affirm the truth of your being in the only time there is, the present moment.

Is there a technique I can use that will help me begin to forgive others? Yes, this process is summed up by the words attributed to Jesus Christ in the Gospel of Matthew. "You have heard that it was said, 'You shall love your neighbor and hate your enemy.' But I say to you, love your enemies and pray for those who persecute you." (Matt. 5:43-44) To pray for someone you seek to forgive is to sincerely desire the highest and best for them. To pray for them you must recognize who they truly are. True prayer for another person is the recognition and affirmation of their innate divine nature as an offspring of the Creator, in spite of how they may be expressing in the world. Seeing the divinity in someone who has harmed you can be difficult. However, it is a powerful tool that activates forgiveness. To set God's grace in motion to bring about forgiveness, you must look beyond the harmful words or actions of another to see that they are acting out of ignorance of their true self. In the same way, when you harm another you are ignoring the truth of who you truly are. By affirming the divinity in the other and in yourself, you will awaken to the truth of your being. When you persist in beholding the divinity in the other, there will come a moment when you are filled with compassion for them. In that sacred moment, all grievances will dissolve between you. This can occur whether the other person is in your daily life, at a distance or even in spirit. Then, you will be free of the error of the belief in separation and you will be able to truly love your neighbor as yourself.

What you are all seeking is a release from "sin," not only when trying to forgive yourselves but also when trying to forgive the other. When you believe yourself to be guilty of "sinning" you cannot move forward. The only "sin" is the belief that you are separate from the Creator and its creations. This is the original "sin" that blinds you to the truth about yourself and your brothers and sisters. Your ego is the judge which pronounces you guilty and sends you to the jail of guilt and shame. You can only be free of "sin" when you realize that there is only One presence and One power in the universe, of which all are a part. Focus on oneness with your enemies and you will, through the power of grace, break through to true forgiveness and peace. Forgiveness of self and others is the healing energy that sets you free from the human condition of forgetfulness!

On Relationships:

Why is it necessary to work with others to evolve spiritually? It is necessary to evolve with other souls because the process of spiritual evolution is through joining. Competition is counter-productive as it is born of the personal, ego self. It has no purpose or place in relationships of spiritual evolution. You are currently human and divine. While in a body vehicle, there will be issues of dominance and submission in your relationships. Relationships of joining for spiritual growth, however, are relationships based on equality. This means that the individuals involved have acquired a similar level of awakening and they choose to evolve together.

One's level of awakening is most important as you seek to grow together to fulfill your intertwined purposes. To be successful, there must be respect for and recognition of the special gifts each individual brings to the group. Some individuals, within such a joining, will be better suited to attend to the physical necessities of life on earth. Other individuals will be better equipped to guide spiritual unfoldment. There must not be jealousies or comparisons made between individuals. There is no greater honor in being a spiritual leader than in making physical contributions to support the overall purpose of the joining. All contributions are equally important. Each person must be thankful for their own abilities and contributions. When joining together for spiritual purpose, it is important that each individual willingly fulfills their role. Each one is like a cell in the body. If one cell refuses to fulfill its function and decides to take over the function of another, it will cause disease in the body vehicle. The purpose of spiritual groupings is to assist others of lesser spiritual understanding to awaken and to discover their own gifts and purposes. In your world there have been many attempts to create such units. They can be challenging and yet, they afford participants the greatest opportunity to evolve. As a consequence, many such groups do not endure. Even though such attempts to join may not be ultimately successful, the effort to join in relationships for spiritual evolution is important as all involved will evolve at an accelerated rate, indeed.

Why do we have such difficulty continuing to do what is healthy for ourselves when beginning a romantic relationship? Is this a test? You love to think of your challenges as tests! The connotation here is that the Creator cannot be trusted and desires you to fail. This, of course, is not true. The truth is that romantic love has become your god! This happens when you misplace your longing for God Experience and project it onto another human being. In a romantic encounter there are moments in which the boundary between you and the other, temporarily fall away. This brings you a feeling of ecstasy, the sensation that joining with another may bring. Seeking this feeling can become an addiction. When it does, you may be driven to recreate romantic scenarios over and over again to experience this powerful, yet fleeting, feeling of ecstasy.

We are not saying that true joining cannot exist in your relationships, however, it does not exist in romantic relationships as you understand them. Thus, when you enter into a romantic relationship, you may find that all the desire you have for God Experience falls away. This is due to the expectations you project onto your partner and the expectations you place on yourself in the relationship. If you believe that joining is contingent on fulfilling the expectations of another individual, you will enter into the illusion of who they want you to be. How can you remain who you truly are while constantly trying to maintain illusions about yourself and your partner? This is a full-time job! No matter how hard you try, you will fail to continually be another person's romantic illusion. When you become disillusioned enough with romantic relationships, you will return to placing your relationship with the Creator first. When entering a relationship, honestly ask yourself, "Will this relationship be productive or counter-productive to my continued spiritual unfoldment?" If it is productive, the other person will encourage and support your spiritual practice and good body maintenance. It is up to you, is it not, to make wise choices in this important aspect of your life. You may find yourself disillusioned with romantic love many times. Your disillusionment will bring you to a greater desire for God Experience. The ecstasy of God Experience is always available to you, it does not depend on any other individual. Your romantic follies teach you. They also bring you a great deal of difficulty and pain. Therefore, seek God Experience first and let your human relationships be guided by your desire to more fully join with the Creator.

On Health and Healing:

There is so much emphasis on the body in our world. There is more done to preserve the body then to evolve the soul. Please comment. Yes, there is much emphasis placed on adorning the body and making it strong. The obsession with feats of strength and endurance is based on the fear of the inevitable decomposition of the body vehicle. This emphasis is generated by those who identify themselves almost totally with their bodies. In other words, they believe that they are their bodies rather than understanding that they are an eternal spiritual Essence temporarily housed in a body vehicle.

Keeping the body in good health and physically fit is important. However, when the motivation to do so is the fear of death, an obsession to perfect the body can be harmful. When the motivation to keep the body healthy is an understanding that it is a temple of the Creator, then the ability to maintain it in a balanced state will be much greater. The body vehicle does not need to display great strength and endurance beyond that which is necessary for daily life. Therefore, your purpose in preserving it is to give you the longest length of time possible in physical reality. You cannot evolve and grow in the school called "earth" without being housed in a body vehicle. Therefore, give thanks for your physical, mental, emotional and energy bodies and maintain them well. Do not go to extremes. Practice moderation in all things and you will dwell in a healthy body vehicle for many years.

You have said that an Essence enters a body vehicle many times. Please speak about this in relation to abortion. We have told you there are many Essences waiting to enter into physical incarnation. When a body vehicle is being created, the appropriate Essence is drawn to the individuals who will bring it forth, thus, an Essence wishing to come through particular individuals may be present in the aura of the female. Essences enter into bodies to learn and to teach. We feel it is best to allow Essences to enter into the physical realm unimpeded. An Essence will not enter into a situation that does not serve a higher purpose for all involved. Therefore, if a child is brought forth in a situation in which it has little possibility of survival, the Essence has done so for a particular reason. This, from an earthly perspective seems cruel. You may feel it would be best not to allow such a birth to take place. You cannot, however, understand the choice of another Essence as it enters and leaves the body vehicle.

The controversy over abortion has to do with the choice a female individual has to bring forth a body vehicle into incarnation or not. It is important to understand that a woman who chooses to abort a pregnancy is not committing murder. There are those who strongly believe that having an abortion is killing a human being who has only one opportunity to live and be redeemed. From this point of view, abortion is a sin and a tragedy, indeed. The truth is that when a woman chooses to abort a fetus before it is capable of housing an Essence, the result is a lost opportunity for spiritual growth with all involved. However, when you understand the complex processes involved in connecting an Essence with particular souls already incarnated, it is best to allow the body vehicle to come forth for the spiritual growth of all concerned. Remember, each Essence chooses its next life circumstances. We understand that this knowledge is difficult to accept, particularly when the conditions of a birth are severe or painful. All incarnations are chosen to heal karma and for the evolution of the souls involved.

Teachers, please speak to us about healing. To fulfill your highest purpose, it is necessary that your body vehicle functions well. You cannot consciously join with the Creator when your body is racked with pain, disease or the inability to sustain physical life. Therefore, it is most important that you care for your physical vehicle properly. There are many strange ideas concerning healing within your realm. Most of these ideas dance around the real issue. The basis of all healing relies on understanding your connection to the Creator through your Essence. We do not suggest praying for physical healing. Instead, we urge you to surrender your need for physical restoration to your true self, thus allowing its wisdom to guide you to true healing on every level. We incarnated once in your reality. For us, this was a necessary experience to be qualified to teach you. We had to experience the limitations of physicality. We acted as the healer in a primitive tribe. Our healing practices had to do with rejoining an individual with the divinity within themselves. They were not separated from their true selves, however, they believed themselves to be separated. We used ceremonies and rituals designed to bring them back into conscious awareness of their true nature. Once reunited with themselves, they could begin to heal.

What is the difference between praying for healing and surrendering to be healed? When you pray for healing, you are asking that it take place in a particular way, are you not? You ask that you or another individual be restored to physical health. This is not healing at its deepest level. When we suggest that you surrender your need for healing to your Essence, we are advising you to put the Creator first, even above your desire for healing in the body. The channel had this experience when she was very ill. She finally stopped fighting the illness and surrendered her dilemma completely to the higher will of the Creator, ready to accept whatever the outcome might be. From that moment, she was led to practitioners who helped her be restored to health. Generally, when you pray for bodily healing, you have an attachment as to how it should take place. The way to make the shift to the true self is to surrender all of your personal preferences. This is not a process of giving up, it is a process of giving over your healing to the Creator by becoming inner-dependent. As you surrender in this way, you will find yourself in contact with a higher wisdom and knowledge. It is through this higher wisdom that you will be led to your healing in its most complete form.

Are you saying that it is not necessary for the physical body to be healed? In some cases, physical healing is possible, in other cases, it is not. For both, surrender to the wisdom of the true self is the path forward. Surrender is very powerful. Some individuals who have surrendered when near death have been miraculously restored. Surrender allows the energy of the Creator to move freely in the body and bring about balance and wholeness. It is not efficient to have to take on another body to continue your spiritual growth. It is more efficient to stay in the body you have for as long as possible. However, sometimes the body vehicle is past its ability to be restored and it must be released. If this is the case, then transition and reincarnation become the healing.

On Guidance:

How do we know when we are listening to higher guidance rather than to our personal preferences? This is a matter of practice. You must practice making the shift from functioning out of the ego self to functioning out of the true self. This can be accomplished through spiritual practices such as meditation. Any form of meditation that leads you into stillness will assist you in making this shift. As you repeatedly make this shift in consciousness, you will begin to be able to discern more clearly that which is personal preference and that which is higher guidance. Sometimes they are in alignment! Higher guidance will not always be contrary to what you personally desire. However, you must clearly make this distinction to find out. To do this, you must be willing to put your personal preferences aside.

When asking for higher guidance concerning a situation, it is important to be clear about the outcome you personally desire. As a clarifying exercise, it is helpful to write down your personal preference for the resolution of the situation. Then, ask yourself if you are temporarily willing to set it aside. If the answer is yes, set your preference over to one side before entering quiet meditation. Reassure your personal self that you are not trying to destroy it! Your ego self is like a child and may cause quite a racket when you try to set it aside. However, you must do so to open up to higher guidance. Your true desire must be to know what is the highest and best outcome for you and all concerned. Be honest with yourself! Do you truly want to know what the wisdom of your Essence seeks to reveal to you? This is a process of trust, surrender, and faith in the divinity within yourself. True higher guidance will never harm you or another, it will never take you where you should not go. It will ultimately lead you to your highest good. Following higher guidance, however, may require sacrificing something your personal self feels it must have. Practice surrender and faith and the rewards for following your higher guidance will be great beyond your expectations.

On Purpose:

Teachers, what is your purpose with us here on the earth? Our purpose, in your reality, is to help accelerate your spiritual growth. This is most important at this juncture in your history as your world is accelerating in its own evolution. Most of you have chosen this realm as your primary arena for spiritual growth. In other words, the earth is the vehicle for your conscious return to the Creator. There are many other universes and other beings who have chosen different avenues for their evolution. Do not think that the earth is at the bottom of possible choices! There is an idea among you that, due to the dense vibration of your planet, you are at the bottom of the evolutionary spiral. This is not the case. There are many physical universes manifesting different types of body vehicles and vibratory rates which are more difficult to navigate than your own.

We are present to help accelerate your spiritual understanding as your planet becomes a global community. You can no longer hide anywhere on your planet! You must now learn to cooperate with one another to survive and learn how to function as a global community. This is not a choice. Those who resist this effect of evolution will find it very difficult to live in the world. You must see from a higher viewpoint to understand why certain occurrences happen and why you have chosen to be on the planet at this time.

Each individual has a particular role to play in this process. It is important to begin to allow the awareness of that role to come forth from within your own being. It is within contact with the true self that this role can be made known to you. Many individuals spend their entire lives, do they not, trying to be somewhere else, tiptoeing through life to be as comfortable and safe as they possibly can. This is not your purpose for being here. Your purpose for being here is to evolve and work. When you leave your body, you will have a lovely rest. Our purpose with you is to bring you an experience of the Peace of God. The Peace of God is knowing the "piece" of God within you that we call your Essence, your true self. This is where you connect with your life purpose. Within your purpose is your service; within your service is your fulfillment; within your fulfillment is your happiness.

Please speak to us about the creative process. We define the creative process as the human ability to create beauty and solve problems in the world. Where do these abilities come from? You marvel at those who are capable of bringing forth great discoveries in science and inspirational works of art, music and literature. For example, how did Mozart compose such beautiful music as a young child? It appears that he was born with this ability. You are correct, he was born with amazing musical abilities but he also cooperated with his innate gifts to have them come forth into expression. You may not believe it, but like Mozart, Shakespeare or Einstein, you are each born with innate creative abilities which, when given expression, will enhance the advancement of the world in which you live. Every contribution of beauty and innovation is essential to everyone on the planet. You need to broaden your idea of what creativity is in order to bring forth advancements, no matter how small. The channel's ability to be a verbal bridge of communication between earth consciousness and higher levels of consciousness is an act of creativity. And yet, for many years she buried her creative gift out of the fear of being ridiculed and rejected.

The key to letting your creative gifts flow into manifestation is to let them flow into manifestation! Most of you confine your understanding of what is creative activity to art, music and literature. The truth is, it is so much more than that. Have you heard the expression, "You are God's hands and feet in the world?" This is true. Creation and creativity must flow through you to become visible in the world. To do so, you must get your fear-based, ego self out of the way. The ego self is the judge, jury and prison of creative energy flow. You may not realize how often you tell yourselves that you are not a creative person because you believe you cannot express artistically. Creative expression is so much more than artistic ability. We urge you to broaden your vision of what is possible to express through you. You do not need to be perfect. Perfectionism is poison to the creative process. You cannot and will not be perfect while in a body vehicle. Whether you are approaching a problem to be solved or a blank canvas, take a moment to set the judgments and doubts of your personal self aside. Visualize your ego self as a little child and send it off to daycare with assurances that you will be with it again soon. Then, open to the flow of the energy and insights from your true self. Do not let the thought "I am not good enough" encroach on this process. As you let creative energy flow freely through you, you will be amazed by the inspired ideas and talents you bring forth.

Is it true that we create our physical reality through our minds?
In your modern metaphysics, it is widely believed that you have, within your mental and emotional bodies, the power to create physical reality. You do have some measure of control over your physical reality, however, you do not have ultimate control. At some point in your spiritual journey, it is best to release the plotting's of the mind as it attempts to draw to you the things you desire. These desires are born of personal preferences from the ego aspect of your

being. You can draw to you what you think you want, however, that which you think you want will not bring you the peace, happiness and fulfillment you truly desire.

Learning to consciously create your personal reality is a necessary step toward understanding the nature of the metaphysical aspect of the world in which you live. The metaphysical Law of Manifestation applies only in the physical world. The law can be summed up by the formula: thought + feeling = manifestation. Your thought patterns and their accompanying emotions affect your daily reality. You discover this truth by consciously experimenting with it. Consciously using the Law of Manifestation moves you from believing you are a victim of circumstances to claiming some power over your life experience. To do so, you must be willing to change your thinking about yourself, your relationships and your world. As you do, your life will change in many ways. You will move from living out of a negative energy pole to expressing from a more positive energy pole, thus, changing the vibrations you transmit from your mental and emotional bodies. As you begin to generate a more positive vibration, you will draw to you people and things that support who you truly are in your Essence. However, as you exercise your manifesting powers, some limitations will arise. You may become frustrated because you can't understand why you failed to manifest what you want in certain areas of your life. Challenges in the area of life you feel most powerless to effect are the Creator's gifts to you. Such difficulties serve your spiritual growth because they will lead you beyond positive thinking techniques to a deeper understanding of the universe. When you make this shift in consciousness, you will find that trying to manifest what you want no longer appeals to you. You will discover that using metaphysical techniques become more and more difficult with increasingly poor results. You may question what is true and become disillusioned with everything you previously thought you knew. What seemed so wondrous now becomes meaningless. This occurs for a greater good as it is preparation to receive a higher understanding. You may feel it is being forced upon you but it is occurring as a result of your own desire for greater God Experience.

On God Experience:

What is Transcendence? True transcendence is the experience of conscious reunification with the Creator. This experience is beyond most individuals' capacity to withstand while in a body vehicle. It is not ultimately beyond your capacity, of course, however it is beyond the reach of most individuals at the present time. You must be careful that, as you seek God Experience, you do not do so in an attempt to escape your current physical reality. You desire to be transported out of your day-to-day existence, believing that a miraculous transformation will erase all your challenges and the need to transform your consciousness right where you are.

There are those who have desired transcendence so completely that they have experienced the tremendous light of the Creator. However, after such an experience they find it difficult, if not impossible, to remain in a body vehicle. Such an intense desire to experience instantaneous union with the Creator is often fueled by the desire of the ego self. Thus, the experience is filtered through the ego, shattering its ability to navigate the world of form. Do not seek transcendence in this way. It will not ultimately propel you forward on your spiritual journey and, if attained, may even set you back.

An experience of a transcendent moment, received spontaneously, will propel you forward without the trap of ego involvement. You may call these moments of transcendence, grace. Such transcendent moments are bestowed, not compelled. They are bestowed as a gift of the spirit when you are humbly open to the glory of the Creator. Moments of grace can lovingly intrude in your everyday life and relationships. They are inspiring in ways that are within your capacity to assimilate into your spiritual journey as it is unfolding in your current incarnation. Live your lives in the awareness that the gift of God's grace can be received at any time. Welcome transcendent moments into your daily life. Be thankful for them and for the opportunities they give you to express the Creator's love and peace in the world.

How can I live more fully in the present moment? When you are in a body vehicle, you often find you are living in a state of anxiety. Your anxiety is born of mental and emotional projections from the past into possible experiences in the future, thus, entirely bypassing the present moment. We call the present moment the "presence" moment as it is the only moment in which you can experience the Creator's presence. At this stage in your evolution, it is common for you to project past fears into the future and thus, through the Law of Manifestation, create that which you fear in physical form. It is easier for you to live in fear of the future than to live in the peace of the present. This is why practicing some form of meditation is important. During meditation there is an attempt, at least, to be open to the present moment. When you do so, even for a brief time, anxiety and fear are released and you are suspended in the light and love of the Creator. In the present moment, concerns and fears are suspended until you choose to take them up again. During such transcendent moments, not only will your mental and emotional bodies be eased but your body vehicle will be restored to its natural state of balance. You can practice being in the present moment during the course of your day by recognizing fear thoughts and feelings when they arise within you. When they do, stop, take a deep breath and affirm: "I return to the 'presence' moment and I am filled with peace."

On Jesus of Nazareth:

Teachers, please speak to us about Jesus Christ. The man, Jesus of Nazareth, was a highly spiritually evolved being who chose to come into the world to uplift the vibration of the planet. His vibration of love and forgiveness is alive today. It has been amplified over centuries by the worship of thousands of individuals in his Spiritual Family and by many others who are inspired by his teachings and spirit.

Over time, the story of Jesus of Nazareth, who became Jesus the Christ, has been embellished and glorified to meet human needs and wants. His special birth and miraculous resurrection are, for the most part, myths that have been attached to his story to enhance his status in the minds of those who need a more concrete conception of the Creator. There is no judgment in this unless these myths are used to disparage or harm others. Sadly, they have often been used in this way. The man, Jesus of Nazareth, came into the world in the usual way. However, he retained the memory of who he was and why he had chosen to incarnate on the earth. He proceeded to let his light shine forth by teaching and demonstrating the higher spiritual understanding he possessed. He didn't incarnate to create a new world religion called Christianity. Jesus was never a Christian; he was a Hebrew who was well-versed in Jewish teachings and traditions. By virtue of his higher understanding, he confronted the greed and power abuses of his own religious leaders, the Pharisees and Sadducees.

The belief that Jesus of Nazareth was the Jewish Messiah, a savior who had come to free God's people from bondage, evolved over the course of his public ministry. In truth, Jesus was a holy man who traveled from place to place with a group of disciples. They lived off the kindness of strangers, those who recognized his high spiritual vibration. As he became more widely known for his teachings, healings and challenges to the Jewish religious authorities, large crowds began to follow him. The Hebrews, who were living in bondage to Rome, began to project their desire for Jesus to be the prophesied Messiah. Yet, to truly be the Jewish Messiah, he would have had to raise an army, successfully conquer Rome and become their earthly king, as well as their spiritual leader. When Jesus remained true to his spiritual calling and refused to physically fight to free them, the crowds, who wanted to be saved, turned against him. They demanded that the Hebrew and Roman authorities put Jesus to death because he was an imposter, not the worldly savior they wanted him to be. The authorities in power were more than willing to fulfill their demands as they were afraid that Jesus would rally the crowd, stage a revolution and declare himself king.

Crucifixion was a Roman method of executing criminals designed, not only to kill, but to denigrate. Therefore, Jesus was crucified on the cross between two thieves. Usually, the bodies of those crucified were left on the cross to be consumed by vermin and birds, a grotesque visual reminder to others to obey the law. However, Jesus' disciples were allowed to remove his body from the cross and place it in a burial tomb. The belief that Jesus of Nazareth then resurrected in the physical body is when he became the Christ which means "chosen of God."

"I came that they may have life, and have it abundantly.(John 10:10)

*I have not
abandoned you,
I am in the Light.*

Lesson 14 - In the Light

The Teachers Speak

Lesson 14
In the Light

My sister Christine passed away from cancer at the age of 69. Although we lived very different lives, we were always close, even sometimes mistaken for twins. After a period of time, I began a dialogue with her through thought transference. I believe my strong desire to know that she is alive and well in spirit, opened the door to our conversation.

I used a visualization to facilitate contact with her. In my mind's eye, I saw a great hall with an infinite number of doors surrounding me. Using her full name, dates of birth and death, I asked that the door to our communication be opened. In this way, I felt confident that I was contacting only my sister and thus preventing the intrusion of other souls who might try to communicate through me. This is why she sometimes concludes our conversations with the phrase, "close the door."

February 18, 2020

Christine: We were pals, indeed. We have shared in many lifetimes and in many different relationships. Soul travelers! You helped me…I helped you. We are apart now for a little while. Mom sends her love and says not to grieve so. She is so pleased to have me with her. She did "dance" out of her body as we witnessed, so joyous to be free from the physical bondage she endured (*our mother was paralyzed from a stroke, she was a dancer in her youth*). Dad is here but is giving us space for now. Relationships are complex here as well. This is the only part I'm not thrilled with.

Roberta: Can you describe your surroundings?

Christine: How can I describe where I am? There is a Light, a lightness to everything. I still have a body but it is not dense nor does it feel pain. I feel wind or a light breeze that helps me know that I am here. Movement is like drifting with intention. It takes time to control this…to go where you want to go and not go where you don't. I do not need to eat or sleep; however, acclimation is fatiguing and does require assistance. Our mother is very good at this as you might imagine.

Roberta: Is there any way you can show me that I am not just making this up?

Christine: Look inside your heart, I am there. I am alive. I will try to give you evidence somehow. Now, I must go.

February 20. 2020

Roberta: Can you describe the moment you left your body? Could you see me beside you?

Christine: It was like waking up from a long, deep sleep. Fuzzy at first, then freeing, so freeing. I was aware that you were there but my attention was immediately drawn to the Light. The Light is so bright and beautiful that it is irresistible, it draws you swiftly. I had no desire to look back even though I was aware that you were having a hard time. I know, however, that you were relieved that I was not in pain anymore and that you didn't try to hold me back for your benefit. I felt a lot of love and compassion for you as I simultaneously rejoiced in leaving the body that had betrayed me so completely.

Roberta: What do you recall after being drawn by the Light?

Christine: Flying, flying! You'll love it…so free and unencumbered by the solidity of the earth plane. I loved the earth plane, so much more than you do, so it seemed unfair to you that I was freed first.

Roberta: When did you encounter other souls like Mom and Dad?

Christine: Time here is a relative thing. Get it? I believe exhaustion set in and I was just suspended. At the same time, I felt supported and lovingly cared for. Mom appeared when I gained some strength. We had such a joyous reunion…so hard to describe…like dancing on clouds together. Without using actual words, she explained to me what had happened and that she would be my guide for the next leg of the journey. I will try to send you a glimpse of us together.

Roberta: I received an image of looking through a long tube, like a telescope. I see two figures waving. I can't make out features but there is a lot of Light. Is this correct?

Christine: I can't say what it looks like from your perspective but we have been waving!

Roberta: Can you see me? Can you see what I am doing at any given time?

Christine: I can check in on you, back and forth. It requires energy and focus so I don't follow you while doing mundane tasks. I have been with you during your most intense times of grief.

Roberta: I have been grieving, not only for the loss of you in my life, but also because you never had what you wanted in this lifetime, a family of your own.

Christine: It doesn't really matter now. I am aware that I have had many other lifetimes that primarily focused on family. It was not my task in the lifetime just lived.

Roberta: Do you know the purpose of your last incarnation?

Christine: It's not totally clear right now… something about forgiveness. But then, you've known this about me for a long time.

February 25, 2020

Roberta: I have a lot of questions but because it takes considerable energy for you to come through, I'm just going to listen. What would you like to say?

Christine: I'm having trouble finding word translations to describe where and how I am.

Roberta: Would a picture be better? If so, I'm open.

Christine: Think of me as a hummingbird. I am constantly vibrating while still. Your heart must open more now, in many ways I held you back from exploring other realms. You can do so now as long as you stay grounded and heed your own advice to stay in control. Opening and closing the doors while lifting the veils slowly but deliberately. Stay true to the Peace of God and you will be safe. Be practical but do not continue to hide your light. The world needs as much light as it can get now. Evolution is a bumpy road. Our little ones *(grand nieces and nephews)* will need to adapt and they will.

Roberta: Do you have any guidance as to how I should proceed from here?

Christine: Carefully and quietly. Let others recognize you. Follow your own leanings and do not be swept away by your longing to be home. I am home but it is not an eternal place. There are many roads to travel. I am not afraid. I am at peace and looking forward to my next chapter. I've got to go.

February 27, 2020

Christine: I am feeling more "whole" now, whatever that means! More normal, I guess, in earth terms. I'm beginning to explore some. Mom stays with me but allows me to move freely. Our relationship is different than before, more like equals on a journey. She is, of course, more experienced here so I let her have the reins. You've wanted to know for a while if I'm all right. Now you know that I am…. more than OK, great! There are some earthly things I miss like trees and food! I don't miss the everyday mundane duties the earth requires for survival. Survival is much overrated…ha! There are complexities here that I don't yet understand, a lot of souls coming and going on their way in and out. There is no need or desire to interact with most of them. Interaction does not take place if there hasn't been some prior relationship.

Roberta: What about Dad?

Christine: Men, as they still are here, are strange creatures to me. Dad is still waiting. I am ready to engage with him but he isn't coming forward. It's best not to force things here as it doesn't work that way. So much of the earth stuff is unimportant here. I know you have a hard time believing that my possessions are meaningless to me now but it is true. You need them to live on the earth so they become very important as grounding tools. You can't take it with you and you don't want to either! Those unduly attached to things have a harder time adjusting to being here as you can imagine. My love of objects had more to do with visual enjoyment than attachment to the earth. I still appreciate a good design, not just in the physical sense! I'm tired, bye for now.

March 1, 2020

Roberta: Do you think much about your last incarnation as Christine?

Christine: Why would I do that?

Roberta: I thought you might be reviewing your life in preparation for the next one.

Christine: Not yet, that comes later, apparently, when I'm ready to enter a body again.

Roberta: Does this concern you?

Christine: No, anxiety has no place here. I am in a state of suspension which is very peaceful and without pain or concern. I'm not even concerned about that!

Roberta: Do you believe you are in heaven?

Christine: Yes, if you understand that it is not an eternal dwelling place. No room for creative expression here, just waiting in a state of light and love.

Roberta: Waiting for what?

Christine: This is not exactly clear yet. There are many souls here as I am here, mom, dad and others we knew. They are all content to be here, as am I. When something changes, it will change and that will be OK too.

Roberta: This doesn't sound much like you as you were in this past lifetime.

Christine: Yes, you knew me well as I chose to engage with the physical world. I was angry most of the time. Everything was so base and crass. I wanted beauty and elegance. You are not like I was; you don't have expectations of the world that are unrealistic. Trying to make the imperfect, perfect, robbed me of joy and sanity! I couldn't seem to get past the idea that life should somehow be better than it was. You always told me that I expected too much from people, especially family members. I was always disappointed. My disappointment could have led to spiritual exploration as it did for you, but my stubborn streak just pushed me to try harder and never admit defeat or surrender!

Roberta: I hope you will be able to continue to report back to me. I don't want to keep drawing you back if it will impede your evolution.

Christine: If I can, without harm, I will continue. Got to go now!

March 8, 2020

Roberta: I'm having a harder time now that the weather is getting warmer. I miss being able to share things with you that no one else is interested in, like my wall hangings. (*Christine was a talented quilter. She encouraged me to create fabric wall hangings and purchased a lot of fabric for me before she passed*)

Christine: Why don't you call on me more often?

Roberta: I'm concerned that I will somehow bring your focus back here and that this will not be good for your next step.

Christine: You cannot hinder me unless you seek to do so. If I can't converse with you, I will let you know. I can see your display of wall hangings. It looks good. I'm glad you have found an appropriate outlet. I supplied you well with projects before I left, didn't I? I know that everyday things must be difficult without someone to share them with. We spoke the same language, often in short-hand. I can't help you with this from here. You must be open to new relationships.

Roberta: It's difficult hiding my true nature, the channeling and this, for example. I don't feel I'm being honest with people but if I am, they will run the opposite direction, I'm sure.

Christine: You must be who you are. For too long you have hidden your light. The world needs as much light as it can get. I can't advise you as to how to proceed just do so with caution and a clear head.

Roberta: I am wondering if you hear anything where you are. You said that communication is by thought, correct?

Christine: You are wondering about music? There is a sort of music here that vibrates not only outside of oneself but inside as well. It is a vibration of harmony… sounds rather than what you would consider music. There are no melodies, just beautiful harmonies…like purring!

Roberta: I'm beginning to doubt our communication. Is there anything you have observed about me that you could not know any other way? If so, can you be specific?

Christine: I see you going to Patty for your hair, still struggling with spending money on yourself. I know you are finding the earth difficult to live in…this comes and goes but generally you are resigned to it until it is your time. I see you playing with fabric. How can I convince you that we are really communicating short of moving objects or something like that? This is difficult to do. Spirits that do such things are mostly motivated by anger or some unresolved connection with the earth. You do not want to encourage it, nor do I. I am at peace with my life as Christine. I have still to understand its full impact and where I go from here. I can't rush it so you will have to be patient as well.

March 19, 2020

Roberta: Are you aware of what is happening here on earth? *(the pandemic)*

Christine: You will be fine. It's not your time or way to leave your body. I don't know anything beyond this. There will be many leaving the planet. There is unlimited room here in this dimension. Try to keep the bigger picture, there is no real death, just transformation. We are indeed together in this one!

Roberta: How are you doing now?

Christine: I am more comfortable. I was going to say "by the day" but there are no days here, just a continuous sense of well-being. I sense something is going to change for me here so stay tuned! I love being with Mom but I understand that this is temporary.

Roberta: Have you spotted Jesus or any other Spiritual Teacher?

Christine: The levels can be seen as temples. The Jesus presence is one of these temples. I have not yet traveled to one. I'm hoping I will…with an escort, of course! One's temple has to do with one's Spiritual Family. I don't think we are in the Jesus Christ Spiritual Family. We'll see.

Roberta: Things are very difficult here and will be for some time.

Christine: Seek peace, you know how! Goodbye for now.

At this point in the dialogue, I began to use the visualization of the "open door" described in the introduction.

March 26, 2020

Roberta: The door is open.

Christine: Things will be difficult on earth but use this time to fulfill your purpose. Being alone is the perfect opportunity to finish your work. Your doubts cripple you. Acknowledge them with a friendly nod and continue on anyway. What choice do you have?

March 28, 2020

Roberta: Please tell me what you are experiencing now.

Christine: There are subtle changes. I am more aware of the surroundings, my place here in the heavens. I see long lines with souls waiting for something. I'm not in a line yet. I am still being acclimated. Mom has left me...rather, she comes and goes. I am at peace with this change although I'm concerned it may upset you. She has her own destiny and must keep moving forward. I am being held in the most tremendous love vibration you could possibly imagine. You are struggling…keep claiming the Peace of God. It is your mission to generate it to others. This you can do without public exposure. As you know, it is an energy vibration trying to move through you once again. Use this extraordinary time wisely. Work to overcome your resistance, it does not serve you or others. Surrender and let go. What do you have to lose, nothing, and you have everything to gain! Close the door.

April 5, 2020

Roberta: Good morning, sister! Anything you want to communicate to me? The door is open.

Christine: Why are you still grieving? I am here in the Light and you are safe.

Roberta: I miss you…you cannot be replaced in this lifetime. There is not enough time for a lifelong friendship.

Christine: Yes, true, but we are still friends. I'm just not there to irritate you and you me! Where I go from here, I do not know yet. I know you are anxious to get on with the dialogue but I have no say in how or when things change. I just know that there is more, a lot more to come and I am at peace with this.

Roberta: You know that doubt is my constant companion which is ironic as I have chapters of channeled material as proof of vast realms that exist beyond the earth. I will continue typing them without judgment and see where it all leads. Any inkling, on your end, of a past life review or other past incarnations?

Christine: You are too hard on yourself; you demand too much. The material you have is not for the masses. It will only be helpful for a small segment of souls on the planet at this time. Keep this in mind when determining how to distribute the material. Your ability to generate the Peace of God will benefit everyone. This you must practice and allow to come through you, now especially.

Roberta: Can you help me with the energy?

Christine: Not really, you are aided by our Spiritual Family. Connect on that level and you will be assisted. Close the door.

April 12, 2020

Roberta: The door is open. Is there anything you wish to tell me? It's Easter Sunday but I can't go to church or out for dinner!

Christine: You find your existence difficult but it is the perfect time to work. There is no time but the present! Making face masks is fine but it is not as important as our discussions and the Teachers' lessons.

Roberta: What do you have to say about it?

Christine: Just this...the souls leaving the planet at this time are being well cared for, even the ones who believe that there is nothing beyond physical life. This fact does not alleviate the grief of so many. You must be able to help with your energy and faith.

Roberta: What faith? I seem to have more doubt and anger than faith and hope!

Christine: Yes, this is your lifetime challenge. How much proof do you need? You are talking to me right now.

Roberta: Am I? Or, am I simply having a dialogue with myself? Have you seen anyone else we know in spirit?

Christine: You are testing me, is that it?

Roberta: Perhaps.

Christine: Mom still comes and goes. There are others you might describe as angels keeping watch over me. It is lovely. Now, back to you! Use this time wisely. Do not let sadness and depression overwhelm you. It serves no purpose for you and for others who need the vibration of the Peace of God.

April 18, 2020

Roberta: The door is open.

Christine: What are you waiting for? Stop hiding your light. The world needs light now more than ever.

Roberta: Are you the Teachers or Christine?

Christine: We are both.

Roberta: How do you feel about that?

Christine: How should I feel? We are one...you, me and the Teachers of Peace, our Spiritual Family. You are a teacher as well;

you have known this for many years. Your perfectionism is getting in the way. I understand, I had the same challenge in life.

Roberta: You were so gifted yet you held back sharing, waiting to be recognized. We both know how that worked out.

Christine: Yes, I had a lot to contribute. I did so in my own way, mostly with family and friends. I had fear of a larger life. I was held back by my fearful personality but I did what I could as I was. I wasn't interested in overcoming my limitations as you know. I see now that more effort in that direction would have served me and others. I was very concerned with protecting myself physically and mentally and especially, emotionally. I was timid. Perhaps this had a larger purpose of which I am not yet aware. You want to know what's happening here…I understand…I have been visited by guides…sort of like introductions. They are waiting until I am ready. I'm not sure ready for what but I know it will be positive in any event. I'll keep you posted. Got to go, close the door for now.

May 3, 2020

Roberta: I have been reading about the passing of a man named Jim. He was very aware of what his loved ones were doing right after his passing. Were you?

Christine: When I passed, I knew you were with me and that others were not. I knew that Jane *(our sister)* had gone back home.

Roberta: What about when I was dealing with your house?

Christine: You were barely able to cope, I was aware of that. You were astonished that I wasn't trying to influence your decisions. I only flitted in and out and felt no attachment to my things. I was exhausted from my ordeal and having difficulty adjusting to still being alive. As you know, toward the end I was hoping there is no afterlife. I think I experienced that nothingness right after passing. I didn't really have much of a religious framework. I wasn't expecting to see Jesus as you asked me about when I was five years old! When I came out of the fog, Mom was there. That was enough for me. I didn't want to be overwhelmed by a cast of thousands! I know you are afraid of being overwhelmed as I was. Your life is difficult right now, there is so much fear and sorrow around you. Keep focusing on the Peace of God.

Roberta: Were you at your Memorial Service?

Christine: I was not there...I was still resting and orienting. I know you did your best. I was surprised to hear about some of those who attended.

Roberta: How are you now? What's going on?

Christine: Now I am receiving lessons to help me make some decisions that will be coming up.

Roberta: What kind of lessons?

Christine: They are hard to describe in earthly terms. They are like "awareness's" imparted by Light Beings more advanced, of course, than I am. This is all transferred by thought and feeling, no words. I am being prepared for something to come, when I have no idea. Close the door now, I'm tired.

May 5, 2020

Roberta: I'm sorry it has been so long. Do you have any sense of time as we know it on earth?

Christine: Your time becomes our time when it has to do with communication. Otherwise, time and its passing have no relevance here. That is not to say that we do not progress...we progress where we are, not through time or space.

Roberta: Before you said you were being taught a greater awareness. Can you be more specific?

Christine: It is like having one's memory restored! Not the memory of your most recent life time, but the memory of your true home in the Celestial System. So much is forgotten in incarnation. Apparently, this is for a purpose of which I am not yet clear. My lessons have become more intense in preparation for my next step.

Roberta: Do you know what that step is?

Christine: Not fully yet. It looks like rest and preparation for new life in the body. The planet is convulsing right now as you know. Those entering will need special skills both technologically and emotionally.

Roberta: Do you have a choice concerning reincarnating?

Christine: No, only those who are highly evolved have a choice. Jesus of Nazareth was one of these beings. The story of being born of a virgin is just another way of saying that he was a purified soul who decided to incarnate once again to assist others in their evolution. There have been others. I am not evolved enough spiritually to have a choice. I have plenty of company on this score. I have no emotion about it one way or the other. It is a journey my soul is taking. Next!

Roberta: Have you had a review of your last incarnation as Christine?

Christine: Small snapshots only, when crucial moments occurred and decisions were made. There is no judgment. It is like looking at vignettes that move! They come and go with space in between for reflection. I do not choose the scenes but I do not feel frightened or dismayed by them...especially those that frightened me in earth life. I see a snapshot and a lightbulb goes on, "Oh, that's what that was about." This is totally objective...life lessons in scenes like a play. I always loved the theatre!

June 6, 2020

Roberta: How are you and what is happening?

Christine: I continue to evolve; it is easy to do so here without the weight of physicality. It becomes something else when one enters back into the earth.

Roberta: Are you still viewing your last lifetime as my little sister Christine?

Christine: Of course, I don't know how long this goes on but it doesn't matter as long as I pay attention and see the truth in each scene...what was really transpiring without the filter of my personality which was filled with fears and judgments about people and events. You will like it here although no soul stays here forever, it is a stepping stone to another reality. For most, another try at life on earth! For some, life elsewhere. I don't know where or what such realms are like. Earth is a tough environment in which to grow, however, I understand that there are places that give souls even tougher challenges.

Roberta: I'm still not sure if I am talking to you or if my imagination is making all this up!

Christine: What will convince you other than a physical demonstration of my continued existence?

Roberta: You said before you passed that you hoped there was no afterlife, just nothing. Is that why you had a difficult time adjusting to your light body? Was waking up a surprise?

Christine: I was disoriented by many things, my beliefs, my suffering and my exhaustion. This is not uncommon, especially in untimely and sudden deaths. Mine was not sudden but it was untimely, difficult to accept, as you know.

Roberta: Anything else you'd like to tell me at this point?

Christine: I am getting tired. It's not tired like you get in the body. It's a loss of energy due to communicating in this way. I will recharge my batteries now. Close the door.

June 9, 2020

Roberta: The last time we spoke, you seemed different, like you are losing the personality of my sister.

Christine: What did you think would happen? It appears that this is natural within the transformation and reincarnation process. I'm sorry it distresses you. Think of me now as a soul rather than a person. I have many facets to my soul. They are coming forward while my personal traits as Christine are receding.

Roberta: You were a very particular and precise person as Christine. You wanted everything to be flawless and perfect, especially your bodily functions.

Christine: Yes, this is true. I had no patience for the less than perfect in a world that is designed to be imperfect in every way. You seem to handle this better, not asking the world to give you what it clearly cannot give. You once told me I expected too much from other people. This is true and it caused me considerable hardship and pain.

Roberta: As I go through the day, I find that I want to ask your opinion about this or that, but it seems you do not care about these things anymore.

Christine: Remember, all the world's a stage! Those who can benefit from the Teachers' Ministry will be drawn. You will not be "shot" as the messenger. You are clearer now about your role as a bridge between worlds.

June 20, 2020

Roberta: Are you happy to be where you are?

Christine: How I feel about it has no meaning. I am light and it is lovely. No pounds to worry about! Actually, no worries at all, just being. I know it must be hard to imagine although you have experienced glimpses of it on your soul travels.

Roberta: Any tips, from your perspective, as to how to live on earth right now?

Christine: Try not to get so overwhelmed. Take one day at a time. Some days will flow and others will be more challenging. Remember physiological things affect you like allergies and drugs.

Roberta: I have a hard time focusing.

Christine: Keep that in mind. Gently bring your focus back to what you are doing each time you stray…like just now. The physical world has all kinds of influences on one's body and mind. Most people spend their entire lives reacting to that which is only temporarily real.

Roberta: You did that quite a lot in the search for the source of illnesses and possible cures. I think you enjoyed it until you had something with no cure. In my mind I still see you suffering and I have that horrible helpless feeling come over me.

Christine: It was my pain to experience. I see that now. I'm clearer as to why but I'm not ready to share it with you. Please stop feeling my pain. You couldn't and can't take the experience away from me. You will have your own death experience. It will be for a purpose; however, you won't understand it until you are out of the body.

Roberta: Are things becoming clearer to you now? Do you have regrets connected to your last incarnation?

Christine: Regrets don't really matter here. I see scenes and I get the purpose for the event. I am not emotional about them but I see them clearly for the first time. There is no judgment but there is understanding and learning…insights that were not seen before. Relationships are complex, most all of the scenes are about them.

Roberta: Are there scenes with me in them?

Christine: Of course, however, most of our interactions were loving and honest. It is the others that I need to review.

Roberta: I think I get it. It makes sense that your life review would be more like a play than a movie! Anything else you would like to say before I close the door?

Christine: Just hang in there. All of it has a purpose in the grand scheme of things. This I did not understand until I got here. Do not be anxious but thankful. Close the door.

July 7, 2020

Christine: Welcome back, it's been a while in your terms. I see you continuing to struggle so very much. You are working things out as it should be. You have the answer to every question. Seek the Peace of God without judgment or question if you want to know rather than speculate. Sharing the Teachers' words will take you down a path you have been on before. This time, however, it needs to be without any desire for things to change in your life or in your world. Living a paradox is not easy. You must stay weighted on the side of spiritual experience rather than in the tangled and tortured intellect. You have a good quality brain, designed to be a conduit for communication from one world to another. You will not be able to intellectually understand everything nor will others. Keep the focus on experience, do not be afraid of it but embrace it. It is what you are made for in this incarnation.

Roberta: Is this Christine or the Teachers speaking?

Christine: We are both. As you know, we are all in the Spiritual Family of Peace. I do not speak from the level of the Teachers, of course, but from a higher and broader viewpoint than yours. The world distresses you as there is so much injustice on the manifest plane, indeed. I was frightened most of the time and overwhelmed by negative energies so I shut the door on my psychic abilities. You do not have to engage the psychic level, even if others want you to. Be patient with them and keep focusing them on the Light and on living their lives from that perspective. Your emotions must be controlled and redirected. I was unable to do so…actually, that wasn't my purpose as Christine. However, it is part of your purpose. It will be difficult not to get lost in darkness, despair and discouragement. Hold on to what you know. The Peace of God awaits you.

Roberta: It seems at times I feel the whole world's pain. Is this useful for anything?

Christine: Yes and no! Feeling the world's pain can either destroy you or harden your determination to alleviate some of it through your assigned work with the Teachers. I know you do not feel up to the task, but you are and you are not alone in trying to do so. Keep at it. What other choice do you have? Wallowing in despair is not an option, that's been done! Gather your strength and resolve and you will be rewarded with a peace you can share with others and the world.

Roberta: What's happening with you now?

Christine: I am in a compound, no, area *(she changed this word because of my negative reaction to compound)* with other souls making the journey back to earth experience. I am excited and apprehensive. All Aboard! What's next I do not know but I have no fear. I just feel love and peace all the time. I hate to leave this heaven but apparently this is how it works.

Roberta: Will I be able to continue to talk to you?

Christine: We'll see. Got to go, close the door.

July 23, 2020

Roberta: The door is open!

Christine: What you want from me I cannot give you. I am in a process with a life of its own…not frightening, but demanding. It demands my full attention and focus.

Roberta: You spoke last time of being in a compound. I reacted negatively to the word compound and you changed it to area. Are you still there? If so, what's going on?

Christine: Yes, this is a place where souls exist in between worlds. Christians call it purgatory but it does not have a negative connotation. I am reviewing my past life with more intensity now. It seems like some kind of strange yet familiar movie! There is no emotion attached to it but I do feel connected, very connected, of course.

Roberta: Any more clarity about the manner of your death?

Christine: How I died doesn't matter to me now but you are still struggling with the effects of being by my side through it all. Do not dwell on it. All is well now. I have a clarity I never knew in the body. Physical life is sure an intense school! We see so little when in the midst of it. This must be by design for a higher purpose I don't understand. I'm going to make an effort to remember heaven more fully in my next incarnation!

Roberta: Do you ever connect with familiar souls where you are?

Christine: Sometimes, it's lovely but not as spectacular as you might think.

Roberta: What does that mean?

Christine: It is like, "Oh, there you are, nice to see you again."

Roberta: So, no big hugs or going down memory lane, I guess.

Christine: No, we are all busy reviewing and preparing.

Roberta: I miss you.

Christine: I know. We will meet again. Close the door.

"Ask, and it will be given to you; seek, and you will find; knock, and it will be opened..." (Matt. 7:7)

The Teachers Speak

A Prayer for the **Spiritual Journey**

Teachers of Peace

I awaken to the rhythm of love beyond measure and joy beyond expectation. O'Blessed Spirit, your grace now fills my every thought, word and deed. I am blessed by the healing power of your love. Help me to release my fears and concerns. Free me from my wants and desires. Find me fully open and receptive to new life in your peace. Deliver me from my own creations that I may behold Thy true creation in its fullness and glory.

Amen

www.ingramcontent.com/pod-product-compliance
Lightning Source LLC
Chambersburg PA
CBHW070852050426
42453CB00012B/2149